The forging, in the eighth century BC, of contact with the West by Greeks from Euboea was by any standards a remarkable feat. The ensuing large-scale transfer of technology and culture from the Aegean to the Central Mediterranean was of greater lasting significance for Western civilization than almost any other single advance achieved in ancient times. The purpose of this book is to acquaint a wider audience with an archaeo-logical project that could hardly be more revolutionary: the effective discovery and excavation, from 1952 onwards, of the first Greek estab-lishment in the West, Euboean Pithekoussai on the island of Ischia in the Bay of Naples. This vast trading settlement is not at all typical of the Western colonial scene. Pithekoussai is very large and very early, and it marks the northern limit of Greek South Italy; furthermore, the earliest immigrants may not all have been Greek. This book about Pithekoussai and its implications is based on Giorgio Buchner's excavations there, which have revealed a variety of component sites so far without parallel in the contemporary Greek homeland. The cemetery, the acropolis dump and the suburban industrial quarter each shed light on a different aspect of everyday life at one of the great crossroads of antiquity.

This is a lively and stimulating book on a subject of central importance to archaeologists and ancient historians. It will also be of interest to the layman.

**The first Western Greeks**

# The first Western Greeks

DAVID RIDGWAY

*Reader in Archaeology, University of Edinburgh*

CAMBRIDGE
UNIVERSITY PRESS

Published by the Press Syndicate of the University of Cambridge
The Pitt Building, Trumpington Street, Cambridge CB2 1RP
40 West 20th Street, New York, NY 10011–4211, USA
10 Stamford Road, Oakleigh, Victoria 3166, Australia

An earlier version of this book was published in Italian as *L'Alba della Magna Grecia* by
Longanesi & C., via Salvini 3, I–20122 Milan in 1984 and © Longanesi & C. 1984
First published in English by Cambridge University Press 1992 as *The first Western Greeks*
English translation © Cambridge University Press 1992

Printed in Great Britain at the University Press, Cambridge

*A catalogue record for this book is available from the British Library*

*Library of Congress cataloguing in publication data*

Ridgway, David.
[Alba della Magna Grecia. English]
The first Western Greeks/David Ridgway.
   p.  cm.
Translation of: L'Alba della Magna Grecia.
Includes bibliographical references and index.
ISBN 0 521 30882 8 (hardback). – ISBN 0 521 42164 0 (paperback)
1. Ischia Island (Italy) – Antiquities.  2. Greeks – Italy – Ischia
Island – History.  I. Title.
DG55.I82R5313  1992
937'.7 – dc20  91–45462 CIP

ISBN 0 521 30882 8 hardback
ISBN 0 521 42164 0 paperback

Alla gente di Lacco Ameno d'Ischia,
vivace erede dell'antica
Pithekoussai degli Eubei

It is impossible to imagine how the history and civilisation of Italy in antiquity might have developed had the Greeks not founded colonies in the Mezzogiorno and Sicily. Colonisation was a phenomenon of the first importance, whose direct or indirect influence permeated most of the territory and population of Italy. Its beginnings in the eighth century marked the full entry of Italy into the historical era, coinciding as they did with the establishment of the major ethnic–cultural groupings and the first movements towards urban living.

(Pallottino 1991, 59)

# Contents

# Illustrations

**Plates**

**Figures**

# Preface and acknowledgements

By any standards, the forging of contact with the West by eighth-century Greeks from Euboea was a remarkable feat. The resulting large-scale transmission of technology and culture from the Aegean to the Central Mediterranean was of greater lasting significance for Western civilization than almost any other single advance achieved in antiquity. My purpose in this book is thus to acquaint a wider audience with an archaeological project that could hardly be more revolutionary: the effective discovery and excavation of the first Greek establishment in the West, Euboean Pithekoussai on the island of Ischia in the Bay of Naples.

Pithekoussai is in no sense typical of the Western colonial scene as a whole. It is very early; it is very large; together with Cumae on the Campanian mainland it marks the northern limit of Greek settlement in Southern Italy; and the earliest immigrant population so far attested there may not have been exclusively Greek. Moreover, our knowledge of Pithekoussai is based on evidence excavated recently and well on a variety of component sites so far without parallel in the contemporary Greek homeland. The cemetery, the acropolis dump and the suburban industrial complex each shed light on a different aspect of everyday life at one of the great crossroads of antiquity. Pithekoussai does, however, have one feature in common with many other archaeological sites of all periods around the Mediterranean: sadly, the material excavated so far is substantially unpublished, and has therefore not previously been assessed in detail or as a whole by scholars other than the excavator and his immediate collaborators.

If the achievement of the eighth-century Euboeans who actually founded Pithekoussai was extraordinary, so is that of the excavator who has revealed it. He is Giorgio Buchner, Additional Superintendent in the Archaeological Superintendency of Naples until 1979. Following his formal retirement, a ministerial decree designated him Honorary Curator for life of antiquities on Ischia, where he began his great work in 1952. In 1966, Dr Buchner honoured me with the invitation to collaborate with him in the definitive publication of his excavations. Since then, I have been privileged to have unlimited access to his material and to his ideas. Words cannot express the immense and permanent debt I owe to his friendship and to his generosity in scholarship.

With Dr Buchner's full support, the first edition of this book was written in Italian for Mario Torelli's *Archeologia* series: *L'Alba della Magna Grecia*, published by Longanesi & C., Milan in 1984, of which the following pages contain an adapted, amplified and updated translation. The title of the Italian version was not chosen by me. I firmly believe that the episode treated here is, as I wrote nearly twenty years ago, 'commercial in tone, Euboean in origin and essentially apart from subsequent Western Greek history' (Ridgway 1973, 5, and cf. Andrewes 1967, 49: 'the main wave of agricultural colonization begins later, in the 730s'). Even if this was not the case, I would not presume to use what D. Musti (1990,184) has called the 'picturesque image' of *The Dawn* (*L'Alba*), associated for all time in the minds of English readers with V. G. Childe's *Dawn of European Civilization* (1925) and ultimately with the seminal *Dawn of History* (1911) by Childe's Oxford teacher J. L. Myres. I have therefore given this English-language version of my book the title I always wanted for it, *The first Western Greeks*, in homage to the late T. J. Dunbabin's *Western Greeks* (1948) – published four years before excavation began in Lacco Ameno.

Rightly or wrongly, I find that more has changed since 1984 at the beginning and end of my story (chs. 1 and 2, 7 and 8) than in the central chapters devoted to Pithekoussai itself. In particular, I now attach even more importance than I did before to matters involving (and preceding) Phoenician and Euboean activities in Sardinia. Those who find this strange, or misguided, could with advantage consult Michel Gras' *Trafics tyrrhéniens archaïques* (1985), and reflect on the reasons that led him to devote a third of it to the second largest island in the Mediterranean (Gras 1985, 17–252), and to conclude that 'L'Histoire ne commence pas à Pithecusses' (Gras 1985, 706). To assist reflection on these and other matters, I have introduced an indispensable minimum of bibliographical referencing into the text, and added a new final section entitled Notes on further reading.

The time that separates the appearance of the original Italian and revised English versions of this book, though long, is much shorter than the interval that elapsed between the submission of the manuscript and illustrations of Dr Buchner's and my *Pithekoussai 1* (graves 1–723, excavated 1952–61) to the Accademia Nazionale dei Lincei (October 1979) and the arrival of the first instalment of its first proofs (July 1990). Nor have these years been happy ones either for British Universities or, latterly, for the Archaeological Superintendency in Naples. Throughout what has sometimes seemed to be a Dark Age made to measure for myself, I have been sustained by the unswerving conviction of my wife, Francesca R. Serra Ridgway, that people would actually want to read this book: without her, neither the Italian nor the English version would have been finished. And work would never have started on the English version if we had not had the many pleasures and incomparable privileges associated with the award to me, at a crucial stage, of a three-month Visiting Fellowship at the Humanities Research Centre of the Australian National University in Canberra.

The Bibliography includes the names of more friends and colleagues than I can thank personally here for sharing their knowledge and good sense with me over many years and in a wide variety of circumstances. None of them should be blamed for the use I have made, or refrained from making, of their studies: the defects of this book are all my own.

Finally, I would like to thank Pauline Hire of the Cambridge University Press for suggesting that I translated *L'Alba della Magna Grecia* into English, and for awaiting the result with rare patience. The illustrations are the same as those in the Italian edition, and I gladly renew my thanks to all those who helped me to achieve them: *Pl. 1*: British School at Athens, courtesy of Mervyn Popham. *Pl. 2*: Francesca R. Serra Ridgway. *Pls. 3–13*: courtesy of Giorgio Buchner. *Pl. 14*: Nils Hannestad. *Figs. 1–5, 17–20, 27, 32, 33*: drawn by Jane Blair (and in some cases adjusted for this edition by Gordon Thomas) to my specifications or after the originals indicated. *Figs. 6–16, 21–6, 28–31, 38*: courtesy of Giorgio Buchner, drawn by Fritz Gehrke. *Fig. 34*: redrawn by Fritz Gehrke. *Figs. 35–7*: drawn by Patricia Mallett for the Quattro Fontanili (Veii) reports in *Notizie degli Scavi*. The translations of short passages from the *Odyssey* on pp. 42, 56, 57–8 are by Walter Shewring (World's Classics edition, Oxford University Press, 1980); those from the *Iliad* on pp. 50, 56, 58 are by Martin Hammond (Penguin Classics, 1987).

*Edinburgh, ferragosto 1991*                    DAVID RIDGWAY

*Part one*

The protagonists

Mycenaean prologue

The first Western Greeks were the Euboeans, and this book about them has two principal aims: to offer an account of their first Western establishment, Pithekoussai on the island of Ischia in the Bay of Naples, during the two generations between *c.* 750 and *c.* 700 BC (Part Two); and to assess the Euboean impact on, or interaction with, the indigenous inhabitants of Iron Age Italy (Part Three). Before these topics can be discussed in real terms, three main components must be described: the topography and nature of Pithekoussai itself (ch. 3; Fig. 5) follows an account of the Euboeans at home and abroad (ch. 2; Fig. 2), which is in turn preceded in this chapter by a brief review of the state of affairs that the Euboean navigators found when they arrived in Italian waters not long after the beginning of the eighth century. In particular, to what extent had the native Italian scene been changed or rendered receptive to foreigners by the much earlier episode of Greek settlement and trade initiated by the Mycenaeans between the sixteenth and eleventh centuries?

## I  The Mycenaeans in the West (Fig. I)

The ceramic evidence for Mycenaean contact with Italy and adjacent areas was collected and assessed for the first time in a pioneering monograph published by Lord William Taylour in 1958. A great deal has changed since then: there is now much more evidence; it comes from a greatly increased number of new and better excavated sites; the importance of non-ceramic items has long been recognized (Macnamara 1970; Bietti Sestieri 1973); the adjacent areas now include Sardinia (*SSA* III), and it has also become apparent that the Mycenaean connection extended as far as Andalusia in southern Spain (Martín de la Cruz 1988). Inevitably, discussion (rather than the production of much-needed excavation reports) has generated a wide variety of hypotheses concerning the 'contact and interaction between two clusters of structurally different polities' (Bietti Sestieri 1988, 23); for good measure, it has even been suggested that Mycenaean contact with Italy was initiated, 'and even carried on, by voyages from the West to

**Fig. 1.** Distribution map of Mycenaean pottery in South Italy and Sicily (based on the maps in Vagnetti 1982, 32–5). The names of the sites in the following key are accompanied by an indication of the chronological phase represented: 1, Middle Helladic – Late Helladic II; 2, Late Helladic IIIA1 – IIIB1–2; 3, Late Helladic IIIC1–2; see Table 1.

*Apulia.* **1:** Manaccora (3). **2:** Molinella (1). **3:** Coppa Nevigata (3). **4:** Trani (2, 3). **5:** Bari (3). **6:** Giovinazzo (1). **7:** Torre S. Sabina (2). **8:** Punta Le Terrare (1, 2). **9:** Otranto (2, 3). **10:** Leuca (2, 3). **11:** Porto Cesareo (2, 3). **12:** Avetrana (3). **13:** S. Cosimo d'Oria (2). **14:** Torre Castelluccia (2, 3). **15:** Porto Perone (1, 2, 3). **16:** Satyrion (2, 3). **17:** Scoglio del Tonno, Taranto (2, 3).

*Basilicata.* **18:** San Vito di Pisticci (3). **19:** Termitito (2, 3). **40:** Toppo Daguzzo (3).

*Calabria.* **20:** Broglio di Trebisacce (2, 3). **21:** Torre del Mordillo (3). **36:** Praia a Mare (2).

*Sicily.* **22:** Molinello (2). **23:** Thapsos (2). **24:** Matrensa (2). **25:** Cozzo del Pantano (2). **26:** Serra Orlando (2, 3). **27:** Pantalica (3). **28:** Floridia (2). **29:** Buscemi (2). **30:** Milena (2, 3). **31:** Agrigento (2).

*Aeolian Islands.* **32:** Lipari (1, 2, 3). **33:** Panarea (2). **34:** Salina (1, 2). **35:** Filicudi (1, 2).

*Campania.* (**36:** see *Calabria*). **37:** Polla (3). **38:** Paestum (3). **39:** Eboli (3). (**40:** see *Basilicata*). **41:** Vivara (1, 2). **42:** Castiglione d'Ischia (2).

Table 1. *Mycenaean pottery and the Italian Bronze Age: phases.*

| Phase | Mycenaean pottery | Chronology | Italian Bronze Age |
|---|---|---|---|
| | Middle Helladic | $-1550$ | |
| 1 | Late Helladic I | $1550-1500$ | |
| | Late Helladic II | $1500-1425$ | Middle |
| | Late Helladic IIIA1 | $1425-1400$ | |
| 2 | Late Helladic IIIA2 | $1400-1300$ | |
| | Late Helladic IIIB1-2 | $1300-1200$ | Recent |
| 3 | Late Helladic IIIC1-2 | $1200-1050$ | Final (to 900) |

the Mycenaean centres rather than the other way about' (Dickinson 1986, 274). In addition, physico-chemical techniques of pottery analysis are beginning to produce interesting and informative results concerning the place of manufacture of Mycenaean vases found in the West (Jones 1986); the distinction between items made by Mycenaeans at home and abroad is especially welcome (Jones and Day 1987; Vagnetti and Jones 1988).

For present purposes, however, we need no more than an outline of the three phases (see Table 1) in the arrival of Mycenaean material in Italy, Sicily and Sardinia that were identified by L. Vagnetti (1982, 9–31). It must be stressed that the Mycenaean pottery dates shown in Table 1 are approximate (see also Mountjoy 1986, 8), and refer in any case to the Aegean. In addition, as Vagnetti herself has frequently insisted, the classification of the Mycenaean sherds encountered in Italian contexts is often far from easy.

In the *first phase* (sixteenth to fifteenth centuries), a limited quantity of imported Mycenaean pottery is found on sites in the following areas: Apulia (the first landfall for ships sailing to the West), both along the Adriatic coast from the Gargano promontory southwards and around the Gulf of Taranto; in the Aeolian or Lipari Islands off north-east Sicily; and on Vivara, the small island in the Bay of Naples between Ischia and Procida. This phase corresponds to the emergence of the Mycenaeans as the dominant group in mainland Greece. The fact that the Mycenaeans' early foreign relations were primarily with the West probably reflects both the urgent need for new sources of metal and the Minoan domination of Aegean contact with the East that continued until the end of the Late Helladic II period: for the Mycenaeans in their formative stage, access to the southerly part of the Tyrrhenian coast was simply the easiest option available. As in the case of the Euboeans later on, the study of the Mycenaeans abroad is capable of illuminating their activities and priorities at home.

The *second phase* (fourteenth to thirteenth centuries) sees extensive developments in existing Mycenaean interests in Apulia, the Aeolian

Islands and the Bay of Naples, where Vivara is now joined by nearby
Castiglione on Ischia (Taylour 1958, 7–9). In addition, finds from several
sites of the indigenous Sicilian Middle Bronze Age Thapsos culture around
Syracuse indicate the opening-up of a new area of Mycenaean interest in
south-east Sicily (Leighton 1985). A series of major discoveries in recent
years shows that the same is true of two other zones: the Ionian coast of
Basilicata (Termitito) and Calabria (Broglio di Trebisacce); and the south-
western coast of Sardinia (Sarroch on the western arm of the Gulf of
Cagliari). In Sardinia, too, a handful of Late Helladic IIIB sherds is all that
remains of what had clearly been a major site in the vicinity of Orosei on
the east coast (Lo Schiavo et al. 1980, 371–9); regrettably unidentified, it is
said to have yielded six bronze swords, gold rings and helmet fragments. In
the peninsula, isolated finds of Mycenaean material in well-documented
native contexts on the Tyrrhenian coast of Calabria, in Latium (Angle and
Zarattini 1987), the hinterland of Southern Etruria and elsewhere suggest
that there may be further surprises in store – perhaps under the significant
heading of exchanges with the interior involving goods brought by sea to
the coastal reception points.

The considerable quantity of imported material in the second phase
makes it possible to compare and contrast the Western distribution patterns
characteristic of Late Helladic IIIA and IIIB. Material of the earlier phase
is well represented on the sites in Apulia, the Aeolian Islands, Vivara in the
Bay of Naples, south-east Sicily and the Ionian coast of Calabria (Broglio
di Trebisacce). In IIIB, there are distinct changes of emphasis: a large-scale
Sardinian operation is inaugurated; imports to south-east Sicily decrease
sharply, while there is a rise in the amount of imported material encountered on the Aeolian sites, Vivara and along the Ionian coast – where
Broglio di Trebisacce is now joined by Termitito. Before the end of the
thirteenth century, the local Bronze Age (Milazzese) culture of the Aeolian
Islands is in decline: this probably means that Vivara now became the focus
for Mycenaean attention to the Tyrrhenian coast of the peninsula. Considered as a whole, the second phase of Mycenaean contact with the West
corresponds to the full flowering of the palace-based Mycenaean civilization at home in Greece, coinciding with the maximum extent of Mycenaean
enterprise in the Aegean and the East. Following the collapse of the Minoan monopoly, there is now abundant evidence for a Mycenaean presence in
Crete, the Dodecanese, Egypt, Cyprus, Anatolia and the Levant generally.

In the *third phase* (twelfth to eleventh centuries), the Italian distribution
of Mycenaean material points to a connection with south-east Sicily and
the Aeolian Islands that can only be defined as exiguous, while that with
the peninsula is centred on the Apulian coast east of the Gulf of Taranto,
continuing along the Ionian coast (Termitito and Broglio di Trebisacce); the

quantity and quality of the finds in the Nuraghe Antigori at Sarroch indicate a Sardinian counterpart to this significant concentration. No IIIC material has been reported from the current excavations on Vivara. The hint of internal transmission from the coastal sites, already possible in the previous phase, now seems to be firmer: a few fragments of IIIC pottery have been recovered from sites in the hinterland of both Campania and Southern Etruria; and the cautious identification as IIIC of a stray sherd from Pozzo-maggiore near Bonu Ighinu (province of Sassari) suggests that a similar process of internal redistribution may have been at work in contemporary Sardinia (Lo Schiavo and Vagnetti 1986). In the far north of the peninsula, South Italian manufacture has been postulated for a painted sherd of IIIC type found in the Fondo Paviani locality near Torretta di Legnano, about 40 km south-east of Verona. North Italy is also the source of a stone axe-mould that found its way to Mycenae itself (Childe 1960); it is tempting to see the first stage of its long voyage in terms of native hand-to-hand trade down the peninsula stimulated by the Mycenaean presence in Apulia. In Greece, meanwhile, the twelfth and eleventh centuries are a period of decline and fall, destruction of palaces, contraction of trade – and emigra-tion, notably in the direction of Cyprus: the beginning, in other words, of the Greek Dark Age.

The above bald account of the extent to which approximately datable Mycenaean material – mainly ceramic – was distributed over South Italy and the adjacent islands clearly conceals a complex reality: a reality, more-over, that was in existence with changes in emphasis for more than half a millennium between the sixteenth and the eleventh centuries. The full geographical distribution and density of Mycenaean operations in Italy are still not clear: to be frank, the relevant archaeological evidence is currently accumulating in quantities and at a rate that combine to defy synthesis. Only a few weeks after he had discovered the first Mycenaean pottery at Broglio di Trebisacce, the excavator drily observed:

the only [Calabrian] site that has yielded fragments of Mycenaean pottery ... is also the only one where the Bronze Age levels have been excavated systematically. Similarly, Mycenaean sherds have been recovered at Luni sul Mignone, San Giove-nale, Monte Rovello and perhaps at Narce in Southern Etruria – there too, these are the only four Middle and Recent Bronze Age sites that have been excavated on a reasonably large scale. (Peroni 1979a, 2)

Nevertheless, as has been indicated, there is a basic distinction in the peninsula, and perhaps also in Sardinia, between primary (coastal) and secondary (inland) reception points. This poses a series of vital questions: the number of actual Mycenaean residents involved at any given stage, the precise nature of (and thinking behind) the activities in which they were engaged – and above all their relationship with the native peoples of Italy, and the long-term effect on the latter of centuries of apparently peaceful cohabitation with representatives of the contemporary but very different culture of the Aegean.

## 2  Italy at the beginning of the Iron Age

By the time of the Euboeans' arrival in the West at the beginning of the eighth century, the cultural state of Iron Age Italy may conveniently be expressed as a series of primarily regional phenomena: three of the regions most deeply affected by the Euboean episode – Campania, Latium vetus and Southern Etruria – will be reviewed in chapter 7. There, we shall see that the outward and visible signs of indigenous Iron Age culture vary considerably between these areas and, within each area, literally from site to site. The differences in question, perceptible in terms of the local specialized forms characteristic of Iron Age metallurgical production, are symptomatic of a cantonal condition at the beginning of the Italian Iron Age that resembles nothing so much as that of the historical Etruscan civilization itself. Artefact typology plays an important role in the detection and evaluation of these matters, for the accurate definition of types is the only reliable guide to the definition of close parallels for individual items in different areas, and hence to the appropriately informed consideration – chronological, historical, social and economic – of the synchronisms they represent.

The essentially regional framework that determined the course of Italian proto-history in the Iron Age developed gradually in the three centuries (twelfth to tenth) which in the conventional chronological sequence make up the Final Bronze Age: and this development amounts to an authentic reversion. Prior to the early twelfth century, the brief period that began in the late fourteenth century saw the creation of a remarkable degree of typological uniformity in the metallurgical production of the Italian peninsula, Central Europe and the Aegean (Müller-Karpe 1962; Snodgrass 1965). The rise of this *koiné* and the rapidity of its effect on the cultural record of a vast geographical area has been attributed to the extent of the Mycenaean commercial 'empire' – which, as we saw in the previous section, reached its zenith in the thirteenth century, coinciding in the Italian sequence with the Recent Bronze Age. By the same token, the swift dissolution of the *koiné* and the consequent return to specialized production on a regional basis were provoked by the collapse of Mycenaean greatness and the inception of the Greek Dark Age at the beginning of the twelfth century (Peroni 1979b).

It is against this background that metallurgy provides a technological yardstick for the assessment of certain overall tendencies which, from now onwards, tend to distinguish the cultural development of Central and Southern Italy from that in the North – a divergence of prime historical significance, of which the first signs are exemplified by the continued preference in Northern Italy for the European-style long cavalry sword, while Central and Southern Italy develop a short sword that is more suitable for hand-to-hand fighting (Bianco Peroni 1970). Differences in military technology are symptomatic of social differences in the areas concerned: and developments in the structure of society, once achieved, are perhaps less likely to be changed or abandoned than those of a technological nature. It has to be – and indeed has been – admitted that the thirteenth and early twelfth centuries saw the rise of at least four urban communities in Apulia, that these townships 'arose as a direct result of trade with the Aegean world' and that 'they would not have arisen without it' (Whitehouse 1973, 623). No such development is attested in the North – for example in the contemporary Po Valley, where Bologna (the future Etruscan city of Felsina) should be aligned with Central Italy. It seems reasonable to postulate a connection, however remote, between this very different experience of the Italian Recent Bronze Age and the differing rhythms and modes of subsequent proto-urban and urban progress in the two areas. In the vacuum created by the effective disappearance of active Mycenaean involvement, the peninsula as a whole appears to owe its cultural allegiance more to Central Europe than to the Mediterranean: R. Peroni (1979b) once suggested that, at the end of the Recent Bronze Age, the cultural boundary between the European Urnfield and the Mediterranean worlds actually slips from the Po Valley to the northern coasts of Sicily. There is no need to interpret the signs of this cultural realignment in terms of substantial southwards movement across the Alps of Urnfield folk intent on spreading the cremation rite in Italy – where it had already been adopted, with varying degrees of alacrity, in some areas during the later part of the Middle Bronze Age (Fugazzola Delpino 1976, 289). It is enough to bear in mind that there may well have been Italian Final Bronze Age contacts with some of the cultures in the transalpine Urnfield world (itself hardly uniform and united), and that these could have lead to exchanges – not least of ideas.

Recent years have witnessed the crystallization of a majority view in favour of cultural continuity between the Final Bronze and Early Iron Ages of the Italian peninsula – and in favour, too, of continuity between the Recent and Final Bronze Ages. 'Invasion' from the area north of the Alps has been discarded as an explanation of change, most notably in the attempt to identify and to account for the exotic origin of the diverse material and societal elements that eventually characterized the historical civilizations of the Etruscans and of their Italic neighbours. We shall return to these problems at the end of this book; meanwhile, we may note that the regional cultures of the Italian Iron Age, the end product of the processes outlined in both sections of this brief prologue, form the basis of the ethnic definitions made by the earliest writers of history. Such definitions were based on evidence perceived from outside: the earliest sources of the surviving external perceptions were Greek, and the circumstances that made them possible may now be considered.

The Euboeans at home and abroad

In the West the peoples with whom the Greeks came into contact were at a more primitive stage of development than they themselves; in the East, for a long time and in many respects, the position was the reverse.
(Sir John Beazley, *Foreword* to Dunbabin 1957)

## 1 Introduction

In a period and area devoid of contemporary written records, archaeological evidence has a special importance that goes far beyond the aesthetic qualities inherent in any given artefact or class of artefacts. This is particularly true when the ebb and flow of relationships between specific areas have to be examined. It is not only the material itself (the actual potsherds and safety-pins) that is informative: careful examination of the associated contexts (tombs, temples, houses and so on) leads to the recognition of patterns in which individual artefact-types regularly occur. If changes in these patterns are correlated with evidence for the passing of time (which does not always take the form of vertical stratigraphy), then something approaching a continuous narrative can be built up.

The following brief account of the Euboeans at home and abroad from the late tenth century onwards consists almost entirely of deductions from archaeological evidence, much of it recently and competently excavated. It is reasonable to suppose that some relevant classes of artefact were made in Euboea and exported, and that others were made elsewhere and imported to Euboea. Naturally, not all these exported and imported goods have survived; and those that have (not all of which have been found) were not always exported or imported for their own sake – any more than Scotch whisky bottles are today, however vital they may be as an indication of the authentic origin of their contents. Concerning the distinction between exports and imports, it must be admitted that the educated guess reigns supreme in this chapter – as indeed it does in most of this book. We have, it must be stressed again, no contemporary written accounts of the circumstances that governed the exchanges involved; nor can we always be sure of the nationality of the carriers who effected them. Furthermore, different

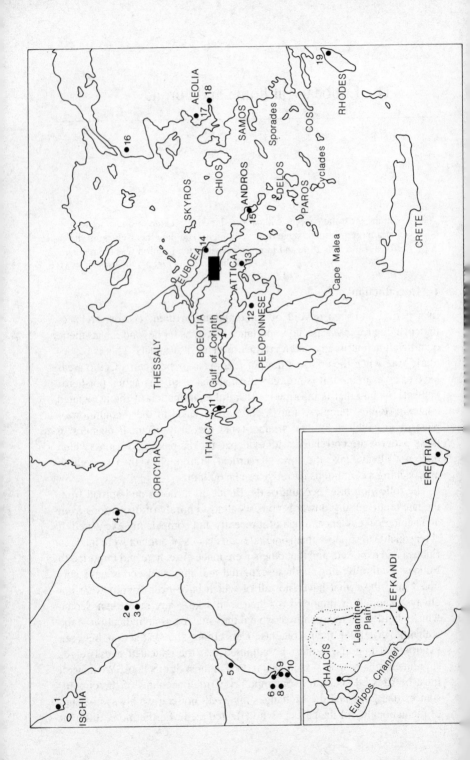

types of context clearly attracted different classes of artefact: it is not at all easy to assess the precise relationship between two areas if the evidence in one comes from tombs and that in the other from houses (or warehouses).

In sum, this chapter will make it clear that we are dealing with an important episode of Greek history: and it should also become apparent that the evidence on which historical reconstruction depends is more susceptible to the interpretative techniques of the pre- or proto-historian than to those of the historian. There is, alas, no Euboean equivalent of Camoens' *Lusiads*, the national epic of Portugal, and of all that it gives us of the atmosphere in which the Portuguese flag and faith were spread across the globe from Brazil to Japan in the wake of the fifteenth-century AD quest for spices. The ethnographic parallel is attractive, not least because both the Euboeans and the Portuguese exhausted themselves in the process of discovery. An important difference resides in the increasing probability that, as will be shown in the third and fourth sections of this chapter, the Euboeans of the eighth century BC were not so much opening up new markets as inserting themselves in a pre-existing Cypro-Levantine commercial network that had kept East-West routes open throughout the Greek Dark Age. Nevertheless, when we read that 'the fleet that had brought [the Chalcidians] from their homeland made them much respected along the [Campanian] coast' (Livy 8.22.5–6; ch. 3.1, below), it is logical to suppose that the great Portuguese admirals like Bartolomeu Dias and Vasco da Gama – to say nothing of Prince Henry the Navigator himself – had their ancient Euboean counterparts. Sadly, however, the human element is lacking in a story that was obviously rich in human interest; the only (presumably) Euboean personal name attested at eighth-century Pithekoussai occurs in an incomplete potter's signature (Fig. 26, lower: ... *inos*). English readers may care to reflect that if their own early history were equally text-free, they would know nothing of the rank, name and proclivities of King Edward the Confessor: as Stuart Piggott once pointed out, they could at most postulate the existence of 'a late Scratched-ware chieftain'.

## 2  The Euboeans at home

Euboea extends for 176 km south-east of the landlocked Gulf of Volos in Thessaly. Never more than 50 km in breadth, and on occasion as narrow as

**Fig. 2.** Euboea and the Mediterranean: main sites.
**1:** Cumae (Kyme; Campania). **2:** Francavilla Marittima. **3:** Sybaris. **4:** Otranto. **5:** Naxos (Sicily). **6:** Leontini. **7:** Megara Hyblaea. **8:** Pantalica. **9:** Thapsos. **10:** Syracuse. **11:** Aetos. **12:** Corinth. **13:** Athens. **14:** Kyme (Euboea). **15:** Zagora. **16:** Troy. **17:** Kyme (Aeolia). **18:** Smyrna. **19:** Ialysos.

7 km, the island lies diagonally off the east coast of Boeotia to the north and of Attica to the south. Its position thus guarantees a safe inner passage – not unlike Long Island Sound, off the mainland of New York State – for sea traffic passing between Athens and the North Aegean. In addition, Euboea stands at the westerly end of various natural island-hopping routes between Central Greece and western Asia Minor (Fig. 2): through the northern Sporades to Chios and Smyrna for example, or via the Cyclades (the most northerly of which, Andros, is barely 12 km away) to Samos, Cos, Rhodes and on to Cyprus, the mouth of the Orontes, North Syria and Phoenicia.

In the opposite direction, however, Euboea could hardly be a more ill-placed starting point for the long voyage to the 'Far West' with which this book is primarily concerned. As Odysseus plans to leave Scheria (probably Corcyra, modern Corfu) for Ithaca, Alcinous cites Euboea's dramatic status as 'the furthest point of all' from his destination (*Odyssey*, 7.321–2; Popham 1983). The notorious perils of Cape Malea (the south-east tip of the Peloponnese) were a further impediment to Euboean exchanges with the West, unless of course those responsible enjoyed trans-Boeotian access to the Gulf of Corinth. This possibility would not necessarily require a *diolkos* (along which ships could be dragged overland); and it might help to account for the evidently close relationship between Euboea and Corinth at the beginning of their respective westerly initiatives, represented simultaneously at Pithekoussai on the Bay of Naples and at Otranto on the Salentine peninsula of Apulia (D'Andria 1984). In the circumstances, it is worth noting that at one point the Boeotian mainland is separated from Euboea only by the 39 m of the Euripus channel. On the Euboean side, this navigable strait is dominated by the site of ancient and modern Chalcis; 7 km to the south, on the far side of the relatively small (6 by 6 km) but fertile Lelantine Plain, the impressive mound of Xeropolis, near Lefkandi, indicates another large and well-placed coastal town-site; and 15 km further along the coast road, which skirts a stretch of rocky and rather poor agricultural land, lies the site of ancient Eretria.

Although the territory delimited by the central coastline between Chalcis and Eretria accounts for only a fraction of the surface area of Euboea as a whole, the places in it are associated with nearly everything of note that we know about the island in antiquity – a most unconvincing state of affairs. Of the two principal cities, Chalcis and Eretria, the ancient written sources indicate that the former was the more important. Archaeologically, however, the status of Chalcis can be neither confirmed nor denied: the factors which presumably made it an ideal choice for ancient settlement are no less valid today (the modern town has a population of nearly 30,000), so that Chalcis is the only early Greek city of major importance that has never been extensively excavated. These considerations do not apply to Eretria, where discoveries by Greek and Swiss archaeologists since 1964 have in large measure made it possible to compare the eighth-century 'Euboeans at home' with their hitherto better known compatriots abroad. Valuable and instructive though the comparison is, it should never be forgotten that the lack of information from Chalcis leads to a somewhat one-sided picture on the home front; happily, the balance is currently being redressed by the series of excellent publications of Geometric wares from Chalcis initiated in 1984 by A. Andreiomenou.

The evidence of archaeology suggests that Eretria was founded in the late ninth century B C. This contrasts with Chalcis, where the sadly limited finds include enough Mycenaean material to suggest that substantial human occupation in its territory goes back to at least the fourteenth century (Hankey 1952), and probably long before. This is certainly true of the wealthy and prominent Bronze Age settlement until recently concealed beneath the Xeropolis mound at Lefkandi, on the eastern (Eretrian) edge of the Lelantine Plain. The Lefkandi sequence, investigated by archaeologists from the British School at Athens since 1964, extends to Late Geometric times: but occupation begins to decline sharply at precisely the period – around 825 – that sees the apparently sudden emergence of a flourishing community at Eretria. It has accordingly been deduced by the Swiss excavators that Xeropolis, finally destroyed after hurried abandonment just before 700, is the original site of 'Old Eretria' (but see Popham and Sackett 1980, 423–7); significantly, the prefix '*xero-*' means 'dry' or 'deserted'.

In view of the highly speculative nature of the Lefkandi–Eretria equation, the present writer would like to draw attention to an additional – or perhaps even alternative – set of relevant factors. Quite simply, it would be surprising if circumstances at home were wholly unaffected by the progress of foreign ventures. As we shall see in the next section of this chapter, 825 is also the conventional date for the establishment of a Euboean presence at Al Mina in North Syria; by 750, Pithekoussai on the Bay of Naples had attained its largest size, and was demonstrably capable of supporting a considerable permanent population of metal-workers, potters and traders. Could not the successive contraction and decline of Lefkandi be the result, at least in part, of increasing emigration to the West? However blunt, this suggestion does at least try to answer a question about eighth-century Euboea that has been open for a long time: what is the relationship, chronological and otherwise, between the contemporary phenomena of major upheaval at home and the assumption of major commitments abroad (Auberson 1975, 14)? In other words, when the Augustan geographer Strabo attributed the foundation of Pithekoussai to Chalcidians and Eretrians (ch. 3.1), we still do not know which Eretria he had in mind. By his time, it is possible that 'Chalcidians and Eretrians' could be no more than a literary synonym for Euboeans from anywhere – including those from a site long since deserted, and hence nameless. It will be fascinating to see if future work at Lefkandi and Pithekoussai yields any evidence regarding the possibility that the former was actually the mother-city of the latter; in this respect, it is perhaps worth mentioning the physical affinities in the composition (established by Mössbauer analysis) of some imported Euboean pottery from Pithekoussai with material from Lefkandi rather than from the other Euboean sites (Deriu et al. 1986, 106, fig. c).

However this may be, it is clear from present evidence that Lefkandi and – presumably – Chalcis attained the status of flourishing mercantile centres at a comparatively early stage in Greek history. Given their geographical position, and the general tendency to reactivation that characterized the end of the post-Mycenaean 'Dark Age' in Greece as a whole, it could hardly have been otherwise. Indeed, there are good reasons – mainly based on the distribution of particular pottery types – for supposing that, from the tenth century onwards, Euboea belonged to a loose and probably informal maritime federation which extended from Thessaly to the northern Cyclades, 'a federation which from the beginning gave its members continual experience in sea-faring, and provided the basis and strength for future expansion' (Desborough 1976, 37). Euboea was 'famous for its ships' (*Homeric Hymn to Apollo* 219), and its reputation is confirmed by the sturdy seagoing vessel painted *c.* 850–825 on a local pyxis recently discovered at Lefkandi (Popham 1987). At the same time, Euboea's topographical predisposition for seaborne trade could always be combined with exploitation of the alluvial plains, rolling grassy uplands and mountain forests of its hinterland: the name 'Euboea' itself surely means 'rich in cattle'. A programme of field survey conducted over many years by members of the British School at Athens concluded tentatively that 'all the major arable areas of Euboea maintained Mycenaean settlements' (Sackett et al. 1966, 99); in classical times, the island was a traditional source of grain for Athens; and the export of timber and lignite is still an important element in the Euboean economy – as is the modern brick making industry, based on the excellent clay that underlies the Lelantine Plain. There are ancient traditions of metal-working in Euboea, including an obscure reference to mines near Chalcis (the name seems to mean 'brazen town', but see Bakhuizen 1976, 58–64) which produced both copper and iron; and 'Chalcidian blades' (i.e. swords; Bakhuizen 1976, 43–4) were a byword for excellence. Seventeen ox-hide ingots of copper recovered in the early years of this century off the site of Kyme on the east coast of Euboea are relevant to the story of early metallurgy and Phoenician trade recounted in the next two sections of this chapter (Sackett et al. 1966, 75, note 125). More recently, certain widespread surface indications found on dry land by the British School survey strongly suggest extensive early use of local metal resources. Some measure of confirmation for this hypothesis was later provided by the discovery at Lefkandi of a large quantity of mould and crucible fragments – foundry refuse – in a context of the late tenth century; it included a number of clay moulds for casting decorated bronze strips or tripod legs (Catling in Popham and Sackett 1980, 93–7). Euboea's heavily wooded mountains were clearly vital to her metallurgical development no less than to her capacity to build ships.

New light on the prosperity and sophistication of tenth-century Lefkandi was shed by an emergency excavation conducted there in 1981 by the Greek Archaeological Service and the British School at Athens. The principal feature of the site concerned is a rectangular building of the Protogeometric period, and so not later than *c*. 950, at least 45 m by 10 m and partly destroyed by illegal bulldozing. Apsidal in plan, its mudbrick walls rest on stone foundations; the roof was probably thatched with reeds; and an external row of post holes suggests a colonnade, indeed a precursor of the peristyle familiar in later times. This remarkable edifice is defined by its excavators as a heroon (Fig. 3; Popham et al. 1982a). A tomb sunk into its floor was divided into two compartments. Of these, one contained the remains of at least three horses; in the other, the bones of a warrior had been wrapped in a linen cloak – incredibly, its patterning and texture are preserved – and placed in a decorated bronze krater (probably of Cypriot origin) which was flanked by a sword and a spear, both of iron and accompanied by a whetstone. At the other side of the same compartment was the burial of a woman wearing a pectoral fashioned from two linked gold discs, gold hair rings and a cluster of bronze and iron pins. Elsewhere in the building, a burnt area on the floor suggests that the corpses had been burnt on a pyre erected *in situ*. A number of new tombs in the adjacent and previously excavated cemetery add significantly to the list of contemporary Near Eastern artefacts found in Euboea; among the faience vase shapes are a duck, a bunch of grapes, a pomegranate and a lion.

The Protogeometric heroon at Lefkandi thus takes its place in the catalogue of Euboean 'firsts': it may reasonably be defined as the earliest major monument in Greece by more than two centuries. That it was custom-built is indicated by the fact that it was closed very soon after its construction: high mudbrick ramps were raised against its walls to form a kind of tumulus. The motive for so much labour eludes us. A Dark Age hero cult, anticipating in detail some aspects of that attested at Eretria around the end of the eighth century (see below)? But the presence of the woman in the warrior's grave is also symptomatic of ritual murder, or even of the heredi-

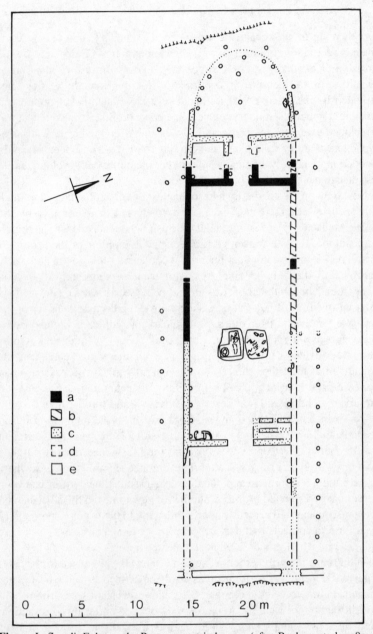

a
b
c
d
e

**Fig. 3.** Lefkandi, Euboea: the Protogeometric heroon (after Popham et al. 1982a, fig. 2; see now Catling and Lemos 1990, pls. 2–4).
**a:** original walls, later destroyed. **b:** wall line attested in bulldozed area.
**c:** preserved walls excavated in 1981. **d:** reconstructed wall line, later confirmed by excavation. **e:** blocking wall.

tary blood-guilt from which – in the grim world of the *Oresteia*, say – religion and society alike require purification.

At all events, the archaeological evidence now points more clearly than ever to the existence in Euboea of a broadly based, well-connected and economically prosperous society at the dawn of the first millennium. We might be forgiven for expecting to learn of subsequent developments, and to read ancient and modern accounts of later Chalcidian and Eretrian achievements on a par with those associated with Athens and Corinth in the archaic and classical periods. There are no such accounts, and it is clear that there were no such achievements. Many explanations are theoretically possible for the decline in Euboean fortunes after the end of the eighth century; not all of them would have attracted the attention of ancient writers, and fewer still would be susceptible to archaeological proof. We have to fall back on the vague and sometimes conflicting literary evidence concerning a half-remembered war waged between Chalcis and Eretria, allegedly for possession of the Lelantine Plain – which to all intents and purposes also meant possession of Chalcis, and so perhaps of the copper and iron mines mentioned above.

The ancient written sources do not tell us when the 'Lelantine War' took place, how long it lasted – or even who won. At first sight, it seems to be an example of the kind of border conflict that is endemic in the classical world at all periods. Nearly three centuries later, however, 'the old war between Chalcis and Eretria' was distinguished by Thucydides (1.15.3) from the usual local squabble between rival neighbours: more non-Euboean Greek communities took sides in it than in any other Hellenic conflict prior to the Peloponnesian War itself. This feature confirms that contemporary Euboean affairs were of some moment outside the narrow confines of the island; and it is also redolent of the practical application of the kind of aristocratic 'guest friendships' described in the Homeric epics. Both these considerations argue in favour of a date for the War in the late eighth century. By that time, it makes good sense to see the material prosperity of Chalcis and Eretria in terms of wide-ranging commercial and other activities directed by their respective aristocracies; individual aristocrats in the two communities will meanwhile have established formal relationships with their peers elsewhere. It is likely that the relationships in question will have been cemented on ceremonial occasions by the exchange of gifts (Coldstream 1983a), the possible nature of which is suggested by the discovery of a goldsmith's hoard at Eretria: 510 gr of gold snippets (sheet, wire and cast) and small ingots, contained in a skyphos covered by a pyxis-lid and carefully concealed in a Late Geometric apsidal house (Themelis 1983).

The actual fighting in the Lelantine War seems to have been closer to a modern sporting event than to a war of the later and more familiar type: one ancient source records impressive displays of cavalry, and an inscription refers pointedly to an agreement not to use long-range missiles – the emphasis was clearly on amateurs rather than professionals, and on cavalry rather than infantry. Not least in this sense, the Lelantine War marked the end of an era. Archaeologically, the final destruction of the already declining centre at Lefkandi may be seen as a side effect, and perhaps more, of the wider conflict. At Eretria, the epic nature of the engagements is neatly illustrated by a hero cult practised until at least the beginning of the fifth century in a shrine associated with a group of noble warrior cremations deposited in the years around 700 (C. Bérard 1970). The earliest and richest of them, around which the others are grouped, has been identified as the last resting place of a 'prince', on the grounds that his grave goods include a bronze spearhead of Mycenaean type – apparently an inherited 'sceptre' (C. Bérard 1982). Like its Protogeometric counterpart at Lefkandi, the Eretria heroon provides a tantalizing glimpse of the invisible cultural cargo carried by the first Greeks who came to the West.

No more than an approximate list of the non-Euboean Greek communities who took sides in the Lelantine War can now be compiled: but it is enough to indicate the origin of certain stable alignments that were destined to have a considerable influence on the subsequent course of Greek history at home and abroad. In particular, the alliance of Corinth with Chalcis should probably be connected with the Corinthian expulsion around 733 of Eretrian settlers from Corcyra (then as now a vital staging post between mainland Greece and the West) and with the extinction of Eretria's other Western interests that is mentioned in the ancient written sources. The main beneficiary of these and of other episodes, apparently spread over the last thirty years of the eighth century, was undoubtedly Corinth – a result that is reflected alike in the Near Eastern and in the Western archaeological record. The situation bears witness to the most obvious aspect of Euboea's demise: after the end of the eighth century, it fell to others to build on the foundations that she had laid.

That Euboea's achievements had been largely forgotten by the time Greek history came to be written is sad but true; it is equally sad, and equally true, that archaeology can give us no more than a pale reflection of them. With that proviso, it is to the most outstanding Euboean achievement that we now return: the reopening of Greece to the outside world in the ninth and eighth centuries.

## 3   The Euboeans abroad

The type of skyphos (drinking cup) with pendent concentric semicircles

**Fig. 4.** Distribution map of pendent semicircle skyphoi in the Levant (after Coldstream 1977, fig. 29; see too the maps in Kearsley 1989, figs. 45–8).
**1:** Soli. **2:** Kazaphani. **3:** Palekythro. **4:** Salamis. **5:** Kition. **6:** Amathus. **7:** Paphos. **8:** Mersin. **9:** Tarsus. **10:** Tell Halaf. **11:** Tell Tayinat. **12:** Tell Judaidah. **13:** Al Mina. **14:** Tell Sukas. **15:** Hama. **16:** Tabbat al Hammam. **17:** Khaldeh. **18:** Tyre. **19:** Tell Abu Hawam. **20:** Askalon.

painted below the lip has a geographical distribution (Fig. 4) from which certain conclusions have been drawn. First, it is usual to suppose that the type itself was evolved in Euboea before 900 – and, on present evidence, evolved at Lefkandi or in its surrounding region: the Lefkandian series published by the British excavators (Popham and Sackett 1980, 298, fig. 8) provides a convenient yardstick against which the overseas occurrences of this and of related types can be gauged and further assessed in the light shed by items imported to Lefkandi. Secondly, this and similar developments in vase-making suggest that, unlike their predecessors in the tenth century, the early ninth-century Euboean potters were relatively independent of Attic influence. Thirdly, the evidence for this new-found independence constitutes a kind of common denominator between Euboea itself, Thessaly to the north, Skyros to the east and the northern Cyclades to the south. In the previous section of this chapter, this common denominator was seen as a ceramic reflection of a loose federation, centred on Euboea, which provided the practical experience of seafaring necessary for exploration and expansion further afield. In fact, a precursor of the Euboean skyphos family with pendent concentric semicircles has been found at Amathus in Cyprus (Desborough 1957, 214, fig. 4a): it is one of the earliest known post-Mycenaean exports from Greece to the East Mediterranean. At Lefkandi, a number of finds from the Protogeometric phase onwards demonstrate reciprocity of contact with northern Greece, the Islands, Attica, Cyprus and the Levant: most remarkably, the appearance of a Syro-Palestinian juglet in an Early Protogeometric (late eleventh century) grave in the Skoubris cemetery predates the Euboean presence at Al Mina by two centuries (Desborough in Popham and Sackett 1980, 347–8: S46, 3).

That Cyprus emerges at an early stage under the heading 'Euboeans abroad' is no accident. It was indeed far from home, but as a base to explore western Asia Minor it could hardly be bettered. For one thing, its own past history meant that many Cypriot towns must have been able to muster at least a few inhabitants who spoke a tolerable version of Greek. Other evidence of Euboean contact with Cyprus at the turn of the tenth century is not lacking. The first known vase imported to Greece from Cyprus since Mycenaean times is a typical bichrome jug in an exceptionally rich Late Protogeometric (before *c.* 900) grave in the Palia Perivolia cemetery at Lefkandi (Desborough in Popham and Sackett 1980, 350: P22, 19); it was associated with two gold rings, two gold-plated hair ornaments (all probably imported from the East Mediterranean) and an iron pin. ·Cypriot taste may also have inspired the local maker of the unique terracotta figure known as the 'Lefkandi centaur', ritually decapitated and deliberately divided between two Sub-Protogeometric I (*c.* 900–875) graves in the Toumba cemetery – artistically and archaeologically one of the most remarkable pieces of early Greek sculpture that has come down to us (Pl. 1; Desborough in Popham and Sackett 1980, 344–5: Tl, 5 + T3, 3). In mythological terms, the homeland of the centaurs (part beasts, part men) was located immediately to the north of Euboea, in Thessaly, especially on Mount Pelion above the Gulf of Volos: the Lefkandi figure might thus constitute a further indication of contemporary inter-regional connections. Finally, as we saw in the previous section, it is precisely to the late tenth century that the fragmentary moulds from the Lefkandi bronze-founder's workshop should be dated; some of them bear a design that is characteristic

**Pl. 1.** Lefkandi, Euboea: the Geometric centaur (terracotta).

of Cypriot bronze tripods from the twelfth century onwards. With this in mind H. W. Catling has argued (in Popham and Sackett 1980, 96–7) for continuous development in local metallurgy, and against reintroduction of bronze-working expertise to Greece at the end of the Dark Age. Neither model precludes the presence at Lefkandi of a bronzesmith with Eastern experience (and perhaps equipment), and both accord well with the other evidence for an outstanding degree of prosperity that lasted there until the late ninth century.

To date, no contemporary centre on the Greek mainland has produced anything like the material wealth and sophistication attested at Lefkandi around 900. As well as the terracotta centaur and an impressive quantity of gold personal ornaments, the exotic finds of this period include a mass of Egyptianizing figurines, beads of amber and crystal, vessels of faience and bronze, and a Cypriot bronze mace-head. It would, of course, be dangerous to make too much of the late tenth- and early ninth-century picture revealed by the British excavations at Lefkandi. Even so, it is hard to escape the impression that the prosperity of this community at this time was based on a fundamentally optimistic – and successful – change of attitude towards the prospects offered by maritime trade beyond the limits of the immediately surrounding region. At all events, contact between Euboea and the Levant continued and prospered throughout the ninth century. In the nature of things, the mechanisms involved are unlikely to have been in solely Greek hands.

At an early stage in the ninth century, the Phoenicians founded their first colony overseas at Kition, on the south-east coast of Cyprus (Karageorghis 1982, 123–7). The Phoenician name of this foundation, Qart-hadasht, has a strangely familiar ring: it means simply 'New Town', and was later used for the North African colony known to us as Carthage. Commercial relationships with the Phoenicians of Kition and elsewhere, acting in their traditional role as middlemen, are presumably responsible for the appearance of gold and ivory in increasingly substantial quantities in the rich ninth-century graves of Lefkandi – and now of Athens, too. Very little, as yet, seems to have travelled from Greece in the opposite direction: whatever commodity it was that the Euboean and Phoenician traders were able to find in the Aegean and export to the Levant, it is not one that can be identified by archaeological techniques. Of the factors that we can discern, however, the most important is surely this: the small-scale and still essentially experimental Euboean overseas operation came into early and mutually satisfactory contact with the much older and much wider Cypro-Levantine network of pan-Mediterranean commerce and communications.

A significant stage in this process was reached around 825 with the foundation of a base on the coast of North Syria: Al Mina, excavated by Sir Leonard Woolley in the 1930s (Ridgway 1973, 6–10, with extensive previous bibliography). Although this important trading settlement was not itself Greek (there is a strong Phoenician element in the earliest pottery), there can be no doubt that the position of its warehouses at the mouth of the Orontes provided Greeks with a convenient gateway to the foreign empires beyond. A few enterprising merchants from Euboea and the Cyclades must have taken up residence at Al Mina right from the beginning, although there is no reason to believe that they amounted to more than a small group (certainly not a colony) within an essentially non-Greek population: even so, their presence helps to account for the prevailing Euboeo-Cycladic tone of Greek pottery exports to the Near East in the late ninth and early eighth centuries. The distribution of Euboean – apparently Lefkandian – skyphoi with pendent concentric semicircles is scattered over some twenty sites in Israel, Phoenicia, Cyprus, Cilicia and Unqui, the important Aramaean inland state centred on the Amuq plain (Fig. 4). Al Mina should probably not be given all the credit for the extraordinarily wide geographical extent of Greek trade – or of Greek goods traded by others, or both. To the south, another contemporary trading settlement, Tell Sukas (Riis 1970), in the territory of the powerful Aramaean city of Hama, has been excavated by a Danish team; and far to the north, in Cilicia, later tradition remembered a Greek foundation at Soloi (Boardman 1980, 50), where the pre-Roman levels have yet to be investigated.

For all its extent, however, it must be repeated that we have no real idea of the nature of Greek commerce in the Near East at this time. We can only be sure that it did not consist entirely or even primarily of Euboean skyphoi with pendent concentric semicircles travelling east, and of Phoenician and North Syrian luxury articles travelling west. We do not even know why Euboean drinking cups found favour in the Near East. Unlike closed vessels, they presumably cannot have been exported for their contents – although it is possible that some were articles of trade in their own right. Others will surely have belonged to emigrants (from Lefkandi?); and perhaps we should consider the potential relevance of this most personal of vase-forms to the consumption of a specifically Euboean beverage, like the tea which brought its own specialized drinking equipment (cups and saucers) from China to Europe in the seventeenth century AD.

Even more elusive than exchanges of (seemingly) perishable goods are exchanges of information and ideas – and perhaps of informants, artists and craftsmen. In this connection, we have to remember that the Eastern peoples whom the Euboeans met had reached a more advanced stage of development than that obtaining in contemporary Greece – which, in the ninth century, was still emerging from a post-Mycenaean Dark Age that had never affected the Levant. Navigation and metallurgy were only two of the fields in which the achievements of the inhabitants of Cyprus and the East generally far outstripped those of their Greek visitors. Under these and other headings, we shall never know to what extent curiosity on the part of the latter was welcomed by the former: but curiosity there must surely have been, and to some extent at least it must have been satisfied. It could easily have been in the East that Euboeans with an eye to the main chance first heard of the rich pickings to be had in the Far West – and decided to try their luck there, either alone or in collaboration with more experienced merchant-venturers from the Levant.

What, precisely, did the West have that had already attracted Levantine interest and was now, in the early eighth century, capable of attracting that of the Euboeans, too? Since we are dealing with a story that abounds in private enterprise, and since we are also limited by the nature of our evidence, we cannot expect a complete answer to this question. But we have seen in section 2 of this chapter that in later times there was a traditional association between excellence in metal-working and Euboea (or at any rate Chalcis, the 'brazen town'); and we have seen in this section that the craftsmen who worked in the late tenth-century bronze foundry at Lefkandi were influenced by Cypriot taste in tripod decoration. This being the case, there is one area of Cypro-Levantine activity in the West that cannot have failed to catch the imagination of any expatriate Euboeans who heard about it: the Far Western island of Sardinia, often and wrongly regarded as peripheral – an extraordinary diagnosis of a large and well-stocked island *in the middle* of the Mediterranean.

## 4  Sardinia

Traditionally, the first Phoenician colony in Sardinia was founded on the southerly promontory of Capo di Pula at Nora. Regrettably little is known about the earliest life and times of this site, where much has been submerged by changes in sea level and by extensive urban development in later antiquity (Macnamara and Wilkes 1967). A single substantial piece of early evidence has, however, survived: the incomplete Phoenician text inscribed on what is known as the 'Nora Stone', found in 1773 – incorporated in the wall of a local church, and thus divorced from its original context; it is now in the National Museum at Cagliari. The inscription has tantalized scholars for the last two centuries, not least because drawings and later photographs of it tended to reproduce the red paint applied to the letters for display purposes rather than the letters themselves. F. M. Cross (1972) has proposed the following integrated translation: 'He fought with the Sardinians at Tarsis and he drove them out. Among the Sardinians he is now at peace, and his army is at peace: Milkaton son of Subna, general of king Pummay.' Naturally, great interest resides in the people and places named. 'Tarsis' might mean 'mine', 'smelting plant' or 'refinery town' rather than Tarsus in Cilicia or Tartessus in Spain: in the same part of

Sardinia, the coal-mining town of Carbonia provides a modern analogy for this kind of toponym. 'Pummay' might well be seen as the name of the king to whom the general Milkaton owed his allegiance: the Pygmalion of Greek tradition, the king of Tyre whose long reign (variously calculated at 820–774 or 831–785) was the high point of Phoenician glory. It is thus at least conceivable that the Nora Stone commemorates a victory over native Sardinian forces won by Phoenicians sent (at the end of the ninth or beginning of the eighth century) to acquire or to protect important mining and industrial interests. Given the location of Nora, these are most likely to have been in the south-west highlands of Sardinia, which are rich in argentiferous lead and iron-ore – and which had previously attracted the attention of the Mycenaean community whose cult place was discovered in 1980 inside the impressive nuragic fortress of Antigori, Sarroch, overlooking the western arm of the Gulf of Cagliari (ch. 1.1).

Clearly, it would be hazardous in the extreme to base a whole theory on one notoriously controversial inscription found out of context. In fact, Cross' reading of the Nora Stone makes excellent sense as a description of the possible events and probable attitudes that followed more than three centuries of well-organized and extensive Cypro-Levantine exploitation of Sardinia's mineral resources. For one thing, ox-hide ingots of copper are now known from well over a dozen widely separated find spots in Sardinia (Lo Schiavo et al. 1980, 379–88; Lo Schiavo et al. 1985, 10–13). A round date for the type as early as 1200 was provided by the discovery in 1960 of several similar specimens in the Cape Gelidonya shipwreck off the coast of southern Turkey (Bass 1967, 52–78). The excavator of this epoch-making underwater site defined the ship as a Phoenician merchantman, and produced convincing evidence to show that it could have been trading with 'Egypt, Syria, Palestine, Cyprus, Troy, the Hittite Empire, Crete and probably the Greek mainland' (Bass 1967, 163). And as we saw in section 2 of this chapter, a hoard of seventeen ox-hide ingots was found in the sea off Kyme in Euboea.

The Cape Gelidonya wreck also contained elements of Late Cypriot III (*c.* 1200–1050) bronze tripod-stands (Bass 1967, 107–9). The type is represented in Sardinia by a fine imported example in a collection in Oristano that also contains a pair of tongs and a charcoal shovel – smithing tools, like others encountered elsewhere in Sardinia (but not in the Italian peninsula), that find their closest parallels in the thirteenth-century Enkomi Foundry Hoard in Cyprus. The Oristano stand is closely related to two other tripods from Sardinia, respectively from Bithia in the south of the island and in a bronze hoard from Santa Maria in Paulis (Macnamara et al. 1984) in the north; it is now generally accepted that they were made in Sardinia by craftsmen working within the Cypriot tradition (Lo Schiavo et al. 1985, 35–51). Indeed, metal analysis gives no reason to suppose that any of the pieces in the Santa Maria hoard were made outside Sardinia: a significant conclusion, for many of the more intricate pieces were cast by the lost wax or investment process. In other words, bronze-workers capable of making (and of teaching others to make) versions of Late Cypriot III tripod-stands reached Sardinia during the twelfth, eleventh or tenth centuries – during, that is, the actual *floruit* of the stands themselves in Cyprus. Sardinia has also yielded the earliest evidence of iron in the West Mediterranean: a worked fragment, associated with a 'wish-bone' handle of Late Cypriot II base ring ware (earlier than 1200) in the Nuraghe Antigori at Sarroch (Lo Schiavo et al. 1985, 6, fig. 2, 5). F. Lo Schiavo (in Vagnetti and Lo Schiavo 1989, 227) suggests that the search for iron, rare in Cyprus and ubiquitous in Sardinia, accounts for the Cypriot presence in the West more satisfactorily than the trade in copper that is usually thought to be indicated by the distribution of ox-hide ingots; it also provides an appropriate context for the early introduction to Sardinia of the lost wax method of casting bronze, available in the Levant and indispensable to the production of the well-known Sardinian '*bronzetti*' (nuragic figurines).

Thanks to these and other recent discoveries, it is no longer possible to explain and date the outstanding feats of lost wax casting achieved by the Sardinian bronzesmiths solely in terms of the presence and example of the Phoenician prospectors and colonists who reached Nora and other Sardinian sites in the ninth and eighth centuries. Earlier stimuli from the East Mediterranean are now more clearly perceptible, and there can be little doubt that, by the beginning of the first millennium, the indigenous nuragic communities of Sardinia were technologically far more advanced than their contemporaries on the Italian mainland. There, we have to wait until the seventh century (at the earliest) for the technical mastery displayed by countless nuragic bronzes. The variety no less than the quality of early Sardinian metal-work sets it apart from the *koiné* (described in ch. 1.2) that briefly linked the European and the Aegean worlds in the thirteenth century, corresponding to the Recent Bronze Age in the Italian peninsula; and the Sardinian bronzesmiths were clearly not affected by the fall of the Mycenaean commercial empire. It is unreasonable to suppose that the communities who continued to require and commission their products were anything less than aristocratic, a definition that accords well with the impressive architectural achievements of the nuraghi themselves. The flourishing indigenous culture to which the nuraghi give their name can by no stretch of the imagination be regarded as an inferior party to the ongoing exchanges with its contemporaries in post-Mycenaean Cyprus and the Levant – with that wider world, in fact, into which the Euboeans pioneered the Greek re-entry in the late ninth century.

The relationship between the Cypro-Levantine world and Sardinia was in full working order throughout the Greek Dark Age. The resulting awareness in the East that the West was rich in metals could have been of some importance in persuading the Euboeans to turn their own attentions towards Italian waters. Where could they go? The Nora Stone suggests that Sardinia itself was out of bounds; nevertheless, fragments of Euboean and Euboeanizing Geometric pottery have recently been discovered in a Phoenician context at Sulcis (P. Bartoloni et al. 1988), while in 1990 the nuragic village at Sant' Imbenia near Alghero produced a pendent concentric semicircle skyphos (Bafico 1991) – perhaps of Cypriot rather than Euboean origin. In Sicily, a Euboean example of the same type has been found in an indigenous collective burial at Villasmundo, in the hinterland of the future Greek colony of Megara Hyblaea (Descoeudres and Kearsley 1983, 41 n. 106). But there was another area, which – unlike Sicily – was rich in metal: Etruria. There, however, the distribution of the growing number of nuragic imports recognized on native sites from the Final Bronze Age onwards displays a marked preference for precisely the metal-rich area of Northern Etruria (Lo Schiavo and Ridgway 1987), Could it be that the first mutually profitable exploitation of those resources was conceived and organized no further away than Sardinia? It looks increasingly possible, and this proposal has the advantage of explaining why the Euboean pendent semicircle and chevron skyphoi (Fig. 34; ch. 7.2) at Veii in Southern Etruria amount to only a relatively brief episode. And so to Ischia, which is a long way away from any mineral resources, previously claimed or not. A few fragments of Euboean chevron skyphoi have been identified among the thousands of sherds recovered from Monte di Vico (Fig. 21; Ridgway 1981a), the acropolis of Pithekoussai, where an early grave summarizes the story of early interactions in combining a Levantine aryballos (as Fig. 30) and an Etrusco-Latial impasto spiral amphora (Buchner and Ridgway 1983); Fig. 13 shows a similar but slightly later association.

## 5 Conclusion

On this showing, technologically ambitious Euboeans followed a somewhat tortuous route from their homeland to their first Western settlement on the Bay of Naples. Nor can they be credited with any great originality in coming to the West; they emerge rather as late aspirants to membership of a long-established and efficient network of international trade. Their situation is potentially reminiscent of that in which Odysseus found himself when he agreed with a Phoenician merchant ('... practised in deceit, a crafty scoundrel ...') to convey a cargo by sea with him to Libya (*Odyssey* 14.287–98; Mele 1979, 87–9); although this tale ends in the Homeric shipwreck cited for other reasons in chapter 4.4, the ostensible purpose of the transaction suggests that collaboration between Greeks and Levantines in commercial ventures was not unusual. We may conclude that the story of Pithekoussai is not only the first chapter in the long and distinguished history of what was later called Magna Graecia: it is also the last chapter in a story that was in origin not Greek at all. That, surely, is why the Euboeans on the Bay of Naples were able to forge an indissoluble link between the older cultures of the East and the younger cultures of the West.

Strabo (5.4.9; ch. 3.1) recounts that the Eretrian and Chalcidian settlers at Pithekoussai prospered until internal dissent caused them to abandon the island. Whether or not this *stasis* abroad was provoked by the Lelantine War at home, the archaeological record at Pithekoussai indicates a virtual cessation of Euboean industrial and commercial activities there at the end of the eighth century. At the other end of the Mediterranean, this seems to be true at Al Mina in North Syria, too. From now on, as we saw in section 2 of this chapter, it fell to others to build on the foundations that Euboea had laid. In the final part of this book, we shall see how, from the seventh century onwards, no small part of Euboea's early promise was fulfilled by the native peoples of Campania, Latium and Etruria. Their unique degree of Hellenization owes much to the second and third generation of Euboeans in the West who were left to their own devices after the events at home symbolized by the destruction of Lefkandi. We are beginning, at last, to appreciate the tradition to which the first Western Greeks were heirs: and to appreciate, too, the antecedents of the 'orientalizing' features in the culture that they were responsible for diffusing.

# 3    Pithekoussai: an introduction

> At Santa Restituta can be seen an ancient vase of pleasing
> workmanship, now adapted to church uses. It is one of the few
> antiquities found on the island, and comes from the neighbouring height
> of Vico, the old Hellenic citadel. They were unfortunate in their choice
> of settlements, those Ischian Greeks. Hardly had a new colony begun to
> thrive, before a playful volcano burst up in their midst and scared them
> away. No wonder the Sirens refused to stay on such an uncertain
> tenement, for Sirens are attached to their homesteads; they prefer to
> dwell near deep-rooted limestone cliffs rather than on the lid of a
> cauldron.
>
> (Douglas 1931, 13–14)

## 1    Sources and etymology

There are not many ancient written sources for the history of Pithekoussai.
The following two passages are the most informative; their authors were
both writing in the time of the Roman Emperor Augustus – roughly seven
centuries after the date for the foundation of Pithekoussai that is suggested
by the earliest Greek material so far retrieved there.

Pithekoussai was once inhabited by Eretrians and Chalcidians. Their prosperity was
assured by the fertility of the soil and by the activities of their goldsmiths, but they
left the island partly because of internal dissent and later because of earthquakes
and eruptions of fire, sea and hot water . . .
   Hence the myth that Typhon is confined underneath this island, and that it is his
movements that cause the eruption of flames, water and occasionally even of small
islands containing boiling water ... Timaeus, too, recounts that many wondrous
tales were told by the ancients about Pithekoussai, and that not long before his own
time Epopeus, the peak [now called Monte Epomeo (Landi 1976): 788 m] in the
middle of the island, was shaken by earth tremors. It threw up fire and thrusted out
to sea the land between itself and the beach; part of the ground was reduced to
ashes, raised high in the air and then fell back on the island like a typhoon, while the
sea receded by three stadia – but soon rushed back to flood the island with its
backwash; the fire there was thus extinguished, but with such a noise that the folk
on the Campanian mainland fled inland from the coast. The island's hot springs are
reputed to cure those who suffer from gall stones. (Strabo 5.4.9)

The Cumaeans trace their origin from Euboean Chalcis. The fleet that had brought them from their homeland made them much respected along the coast where they settled; having first landed on the islands of Aenaria and Pithekoussai, they later decided to take their chance on the mainland. (Livy 8.22.5–6)

In the first passage, Strabo's reference to the presence at Pithekoussai of Eretrians and Chalcidians is somewhat vague. In sharp contrast, the information he gives in a previous passage (5.4.4: ch. 6.4, below) concerning the foundation of nearby Cumae is extremely precise: the official founders of the mainland colony are named as Megasthenes of Chalcis and Hippocles of Kyme. The latter centre has been identified as either the most important of the Aeolian cities on the Anatolian seaboard or an obscure town on the inhospitable east coast of Euboea. Perhaps it is unwise to read too much into the difference in Strabo's treatment of the respective foundations of Pithekoussai and Cumae. Nevertheless, it may be argued that Pithekoussai emerges from his account as something less than a colony: a possibility that is particularly interesting, since the hindsight of archaeology suggests that Pithekoussai was indeed some kind of pre-colonial establishment, succeeded at an early stage by the foundation, with full colonial honours, of Cumae on the more convenient mainland of Campania. This is not a mere wrangle about terminology; important historical issues are at stake.

Meanwhile, we are left with serious discrepancies between the two authors cited above. Livy is clear that the colony of Cumae was established by a Chalcidian contingent from Pithekoussai, while Strabo's version of Cumae's foundation does not include Pithekoussai at all. Strabo further defines Cumae as 'the most ancient of all the Sicilian and Italiote foundations' (5.4.4); and he does not tell us what became of the unhappy Eretrians and Chalcidians who, according to the passage translated above, were forced to abandon Pithekoussai as a result of internal dissent and, later, of various alarming natural phenomena.

Strabo's source for the foundation of Cumae is probably Ephorus, after Xenophon the most important historian of the fourth century, and a notorious advocate of the achievements of his native city: Aeolian Kyme. Given the ideal opportunity presented by the name of the Campanian foundation, it may be surmised that Ephorus would not have attached much importance to the preservation of any mention of Pithekoussan precedents that he found in *his* sources. If so, it follows that the Pithekoussan data retailed by Strabo are abstracted from a source that is not Ephorus: and there can be little doubt that this was Timaeus of Tauromenium (modern Taormina in Sicily; Lepore 1976), who was writing around 300 – he is indeed named by Strabo in the second part of the passage translated above. It is not too fanciful to suppose that if Timaeus in fact mentioned the Pithekoussai–

Cumae connection, Strabo would have omitted it in order to avoid contra-dicting what he had already written about the foundation of Cumae. There too, perhaps understandably, Strabo adds a note on etymology: 'some have suggested that Cumae takes its name from *kumata* [billows]; for its beach, being exposed to the wind, is characterized by high waves' (5.4.4). The same might of course be said of the places called Kyme/Cumae in Aeolia and Euboea: like their namesake in Campania, they too are coastal sites.

A further difference between the two passages cited is probably more apparent than real. Strabo mentions both Eretrians and Chalcidians at Pithekoussai, while Livy refers only to Chalcidians from Pithekoussai as the founders of Cumae. A possible explanation resides in Strabo's refer-ence to internal dissent. Since arms and armour are conspicuous by their absence from the archaeological record of Pithekoussai, it may be that this stasis abroad was no more violent than the 'Lelantine War' at home (ch. 2, above) – of which it may indeed have been an expatriate reflection, leading in the first instance to the departure of one group for the mainland, to be followed later by the other, panic-stricken by the natural phenomena listed at the end of Strabo's account of the episode. Alternatively, Livy may have known the version of Cumae's foundation relayed by Strabo: this has Megasthenes and Hippocles agreeing that it should be considered a colony of Chalcis (the home town of Megasthenes) and the namesake of Kyme (the home town of Hippocles).

Strabo gives two reasons for the good fortune enjoyed by the Eretrian and Chalcidian settlers of Pithekoussai. The first of these is 'the fertility of the soil' (*eukarpia*). It is interesting to examine this feature in the light of an authoritative modern account (Buchner Niola 1965) of the geography of Ischia. This confirms that the fundamental resource of the island in the pre-tourist age has always been agriculture, but in the specialized sense of viticulture, a direct result of the island's hilly terrain, of the climate and of the soil. The latter is mainly a porous volcanic tufa, rich in minerals but poor in humus. The vine is especially capable of retaining moisture, and its roots serve to bind the soil so that it is not washed off the narrow terraces by the heavy rain characteristic of the Ischian winter. Areas of arable land suitable for other kinds of agriculture are few and far between on what is known in modern tourist literature as the 'Green Island' (*Isola Verde*); and they are also very small. A great deal of the island is known from doc-umentary evidence to have been covered with low wooded scrub until the sixteenth century AD, and there is no reason to suppose that this was less extensive in the eighth century BC. The constant fight against the erosion of Ischia's hillsides is the last thing that is required on the broad rolling plains of, say, Leontini in Sicily or Sybaris on the South Italian mainland; and it is no surprise that the 'early' or 'Euboean' period of Western Greek history has long been identified as something essentially apart from the main wave (from about 730 onwards) of agricultural colonization south of the Bay of Naples (Andrewes 1967, 49). Strabo's *eukarpia* may thus be an automatic deduction from Ischia's volcanic proclivities, which were well known in antiquity. Or the expression could be no more than a superficial and anachronistic comment on the island's vineyards and remedial waters, mentioned also by Pliny (*NH* 31.5.9) and Statius (*Silvae* 3.5.104). By Strabo's (and indeed Timaeus') time, it is more than probable that vine-growing on Ischia had been organized on a large scale. But as we shall see in the following chapters, the eighth-century Euboeans of Pithekoussai were intent on trade and industry: agriculturally, they did not find (or require) anything more than the limited possibilities of cultivation that could guarantee their basic subsistence needs independently of the mainland, should this be necessary.

In the passage given above, Strabo's second reason for the prosperity of the Eretrians and Chalcidians of Pithekoussai is translated as 'the activities of their goldsmiths'. The Greek word that appears at this point in all editions of Strabo since Casaubon (1587) is *chruseia*, which is usually translated as 'gold-mines'. But these are geologically out of the question; moreover, if there really had been any gold mines on Ischia, they would surely have been mentioned in subsequent collections of practical information, for example that compiled by Pliny the Elder under the title *Naturalis Historia*. On the basis of Strabonian usage elsewhere, it has been shown that *chruseia* could reasonably be translated as 'goldsmiths' workshops' (Mureddu 1972) – a possibility that had already been ventilated informally (on purely archaeological grounds) by the excavator of Pithekoussai, Giorgio Buchner. More recently, Dr Buchner and the present writer have noted with great interest that although the latest recension of Strabo's fifth book (Sbordone 1970) prints *chruseia* at the appropriate point in the text, the critical apparatus cites only one manuscript authority for this reading; other and older manuscripts have *chrusia*, which elsewhere means 'anything made of gold: plate, personal ornaments etc.' These two possible translations, 'goldsmiths' workshops' (*chruseia*) and 'goldsmiths' products' (*chrusia*), seem to us to be equally acceptable (Buchner 1975, 81; 1979, 136), and I have combined them in the above translation: 'goldsmiths' activities' also reflects the discovery of what we believe to be a Euboean jeweller's weight in one of the workshops in the metal-working quarter at Pithekoussai itself (ch. 5.2, below). Rightly or wrongly, we believe that our emendation of the standard *translation* of Strabo is superior to those of his *text* previously proposed by Ettore Pais (1908b, 185) and Jean Bérard (1957, 43 n. 1): respectively *chalkeia* ('bronze foundries') and *chutreia* ('clay beds' or 'potteries'). The first recalls both the Euboean 'brazen town' of Chalcis and the Roman name of Ischia, Aenaria, which Pais connected with Latin *aes* ('bronze'). *Chutreia* might conceivably refer to the excellent source of clay (the only good one on the Bay of Naples) in the hills above Casamicciola, clearly in extensive use from an early stage at both Pithekoussai and Cumae. But there is no shred of manuscript authority for either of these emendations: in this case at least, archaeological evidence appears to be a safer guide to Strabo's meaning than even the most erudite historical conjecture.

The earthquakes and eruptions mentioned by Strabo as a reason for the second Euboean exodus from Pithekoussai are all compatible with the geomorphological nature of Ischia, which is well known to modern geologists and vulcanologists as a volcano-tectonic horst – or, in Norman Douglas' happy phrase (in the passage cited at the head of this chapter), 'the lid of a cauldron'. In antiquity, as Strabo says (above), the dramatic physical consequences of this status gave rise to the myth that the giant Typhon was perpetually struggling to break out of his prison underneath the island. The recent seismic history of South Italy as a whole is also relevant here: the earthquake of 23 November 1980 afforded all too many tragic demonstrations of the effect of natural phenomena on remote communities, and Ischia itself was similarly affected by the Casamicciola earthquake of 1883. Strabo's account implies a massive release of scalding water: this additionally terrifying feature is no doubt connected with the characteristic Ischian *fumarole* (hot mineral springs). In their normal state, today as in antiquity, they are highly prized for their remedial qualities. So too is the hot sand on the beach at the end of the Valle di San Montano, where Euboeans had once drawn up their boats after the long haul from the Aegean:

Landing one morning on this fabled and sunny beach ... I beheld a sight that froze the blood in my veins; a human head was resting on the sand a few yards from the water's edge. Its countenance was turned from me and otherwise concealed under a white cloth like a towel. The country folk walked up and down as though utterly unaware of its existence, as if such sights were part of everyday life; sedate fishermen mended their nets nearby, children played around, shouting merrily. Shocked by the incredible callousness of the people, and half-suspecting myself to be the victim of a ghastly hallucination, I stooped, trembling, and snatched away the concealing cloth. This innocent proceeding caused the head to burst into broken Neapolitan mingled with a few clear snatches of the English tongue which nothing would induce me to set down here.

It was only an Englishman taking a sand-bath for his rheumatisms. Presently the earth heaved in huge convulsions and the modern Typhoeus emerged, pawing, like Milton's lion, to set free his hinder parts. (Douglas 1931, 10–11)

Finally, what is the origin of the name 'Pithekoussai'? Two theories were current in ancient times. The Alexandrine writer Xenogoras, who wrote a treatise *On Islands* around 90 BC, of which only fragments survive, seems to have derived the name from *pithekos*, the Greek word for monkey or ape (as in *Australopithecus*): somewhat tenuously, he connected this etymology with the legendary presence on Ischia of the Cercopi and with their transformation into monkeys (*FGrHist* ΙΙb, p. 1,009, 240 F28; so too Ovid, *Metamorphoses* 14.89–100). A somewhat earlier writer, Lycophron (who was born at Chalcis in Euboea around 320 BC), contrives to describe the island in a passing reference as simultaneously crushing Typhon, boiling with flame and acting as a kind of nature reserve for an ugly race of apes established there by divine decree (Lycophron, *Alexandra* 688–93). To an archaeologist, an altogether more attractive derivation is that offered by Pliny (*NH* 3.6.82). For him, the name of Pithekoussai has nothing to do with monkeys (*non a simiarum multitudine*), but comes from the makers of jars (*a figlinis doliorum*) – *pithoi* in Greek, which may stand for vases in general: hence the proposal, mentioned above, to change Strabo's *chruseia/chrusia* to *chutreia*. A third possibility may have more to commend it than either 'Apeville'/'Monkeytown' or 'Vaseburgh': it is that the name is simply the Graecized form of a pre-literate indigenous name for the island or its people. Islands and ports are particularly susceptible to this treatment by foreign sailors and merchants needing to render outlandish names accessible to their own alphabets and palates: classic cases are the Italian 'Orcadi' (for the Scottish Orkneys) and the English 'Leghorn' (for the Italian Livorno).

Another name for Ischia, Inarime, is exclusively poetic. In a striking metaphor, Virgil likens the fall of certain heroes in the siege of the Trojan camp to that of masonry collapsing near Cumae 'on the Euboean shore of Baiae' (*in Euboico Baiarum litore*): 'then lofty Prochyta [the island now called Procida] trembles with the sound, and so does Inarime, hard resting place laid for Typhon at Jove's command' (*Aeneid* 9.710, 715–16). Virgil's ancient commentator Servius explains that Inarime is derived from Homer's reference to Typhon's confinement 'in Arima', the land of the Arimi (*en Arimois*: *Iliad* 2.783) – or under Ischia, according to the myth recorded by Strabo 5.4.9 (above). The etymological vicious circle is completed by Strabo's comment on Homer's verse: '[some] say that the Etruscan word for *pithekoi* [monkeys] is *arimoi*' (Strabo 13.4.6).

Aenaria, the Roman name of Ischia, was inevitably connected by many writers with Aeneas' voyage from Troy to Latium: the island lay on his route, so poetic logic required him to pass it (Ovid, *Metamorphoses* 14.89–90) or even to lend his name to it (Pliny, *NH* 3.6.82). Livy's reference in the passage translated above to 'the islands of Aenaria and Pithekoussai' is as confused as a modern reference to 'the islands of Sri Lanka and Ceylon' would be. The latter name could simply have been added for the benefit of anyone who might have felt that 'Aenaria' was still relatively unfamiliar. In this respect, it may be relevant to note that a graffito (*CIL* IV.2183) in the presumably ill-famed Vico del Lupanare at Pompeii implies that in AD 59 certain *Petecusani* were among the hooligans involved in the riot that caused the senate in Rome to close the amphitheatre for ten years (Tacitus, *Annals* 14.17) – one of the comparatively few events that brought Pompeii to the attention of the outside world before the eruption of Vesuvius in AD 79 ensured lasting fame for the seismic and volcanic proclivities of the whole Naples area (Moeller 1970).

## 2 Identification, excavation and configuration

The site of Pithekoussai lies within the modern *comune* of Lacco Ameno, at the north-west extremity of the island of Ischia in the Bay of Naples (Fig. 5). Its identity has been clear since the end of the eighteenth century, when a local doctor and priest, Francesco De Siano, noted the presence of ancient potsherds and broken tiles on the promontory of Monte di Vico and of 'pagan tombs' – clearly Hellenistic and Roman – in the adjacent Valle di San Montano (De Siano 1801). A generation later, the Swiss expert on Ischia's remedial waters, J. E. Chevalley de Rivaz (1835), reported the discovery of red-figure vases in inhumation and cremation tombs in the same area (Buchner 1975, 59). The significance of these isolated finds was not lost on the historians of ancient Italy, who were of course well aware of the ancient written sources discussed in the first section of this chapter. Towards the end of the last century, Julius Beloch concluded that there was enough evidence to locate Pithekoussai on Monte di Vico (Plate 2) from the fifth century BC onwards; he felt, however, that it would be hazardous to assign the same site to the earlier Euboean pioneers mentioned by Strabo and Livy (Beloch 1890, 208f.). Some years later, and for reasons that are not entirely clear, Ettore Pais located the earliest Greek settlement on the chain of hills between Porto d'Ischia and Casamicciola. Pais was nevertheless convinced of Pithekoussai's potential status as 'the key to more than one of the problems pertaining to the earliest commercial relations existing between the Greeks and the indigenous populations of the peninsula' (Pais 1908b, 189). This conviction was partly responsible for Pais' attempt, mentioned in the first section of this chapter, to introduce 'clay beds' or 'potteries' into Strabo's account of the reasons for Pithekoussai's prosperity.

In 1913, Paolo Orsi addressed a historic letter to Vittorio Spinazzola, the then Superintendent of the Excavations and Museums of Naples, Caserta, Avellino, Salerno, Benevento and Campobasso. Perhaps with Pais' diagnosis in mind, the father of Sicilian archaeology courteously informed his Neapolitan colleague that a German architect, then working in Syracuse,

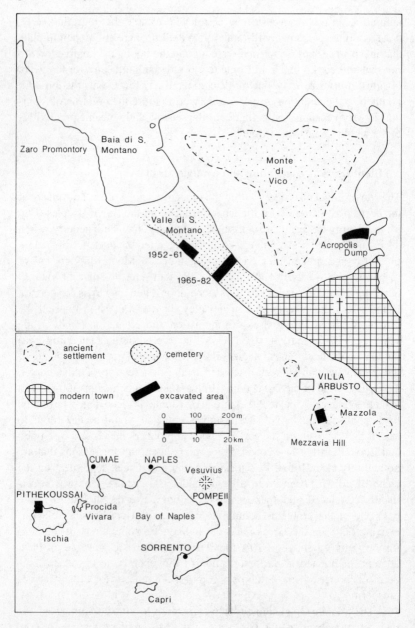

**Fig. 5.** Pithekoussai (Lacco Ameno d'Ischia) and the Bay of Naples.

had shown him a sketch of a sixth-century architectural terracotta 'that he had found on the hill above the [church] tower of Santa Restituta at Lacco Ameno on the island of Ischia' – i.e. on Monte di Vico. Orsi earnestly recommended that the site be investigated, on the grounds that 'it would be a fine thing to discover the first station of the Cumaeans' (an obvious reference to Livy 8.22.5–6). From Rome, the distinguished classical archaeologist Roberto Paribeni (to whom the German architect had shown the original of his sketch) had already written to Spinazzola in the same vein. The latter's reply to Orsi has not survived; to Paribeni he wrote as follows:

The new indication, coupled with the information already available to the Superintendency and generally about this locality, justly reputed the most ancient seat of the Greek navigators (even earlier than their first landfall on the peninsula), will cause me to put in hand as soon as possible the long-awaited systematic investigation of the island, of which Your Excellency so rightly stresses the importance. For the moment, this will take the form of a preliminary visit.

Seventeen years later, however, Amedeo Maiuri could write with reasonable accuracy that the archaeology of Ischia was 'completely unknown' (*del tutto ignota*: Maiuri, 1930). Not long afterwards, in his seminal account of Greek commerce with the West in the eighth and seventh centuries, Alan Blakeway could only cite the two passages translated at the head of the first section of this chapter and echo the hypothesis that Pais had published at the beginning of the century:

The first Greek settlements on the islands in the Bay of Naples (Strabo) were possibly earlier [than Cumae], as Livy indicates. There is no archaeological evidence for this unless we assume, what is probable enough, that the presence of Greek pottery and intensive Greek artistic influence in Etruria of a date stylistically earlier than the contents of the earliest graves at Cumae demands a Greek centre of distribution in the neighbourhood of an earlier date than that of Cumae. (Blakeway 1933, 200, n. 3)

Excavations at Lacco Ameno did not in fact begin until 1952: and over the last thirty years and more they have become an international byword for excellence in technique no less than for the massive contribution they have made to our knowledge of the early history of both Greece and Italy. That this should be so, and indeed that anything happened at all, is entirely due to the energy and insistence – which happily continue unabated to this day – of Dr Giorgio Buchner. With his customary modesty, Dr Buchner himself prefers to stress the element of chance rather than personal merit. Maiuri's 1930 statement (above) would probably still be true today; he has written,

if a chain of circumstances had not taken the present writer to Ischia in his early youth, and if his imagination had not been struck by the following phrase of Beloch (of whose *Campanien* he had the good fortune, while a pupil in the Gymnasium at

Breslau, to acquire the last remaining copy in the publisher's stock): 'Here, by the village of Lacco, Monte di Vico juts into the sea like a peninsula ... The surface of the hill is strewn with fragments of tiles and vases, and intact layers of them are revealed when the ground is scratched with a walking stick.' (Buchner 1977, 142f., n. 28, quoting Beloch 1890, 208)

The following chapters will describe some of the excavations conducted by Dr Buchner for the Naples Archaeological Superintendency in the chronological order of their execution from 1952 onwards: the cemetery in the Valle di San Montano (Plate 4); the Acropolis Dump, the so-called 'Scarico Gosetti' on the east slope of Monte di Vico (Plate 2); and the metal-working quarter in the Mazzola area (Plate 3) on the hill of Mezzavia across the Valle di San Montano from the acropolis. An account of the material found in these excavations is also offered; it is limited to the 'Euboean period' of Pithekoussai, which is taken to end around 700. For this reason, mention will not be made of another fascinating discovery in the Mezzavia area: a votive deposit which has yielded important architectural terracottas (some with well-preserved painted decoration), figurines of horses, mules, carts and boats, together with imported Corinthian pottery dated around 635–620 BC (Trendall 1967, 31).

When the 'Euboean period' begins at Pithekoussai is by no means clear.

**Pl. 2.** Pithekoussai: the acropolis, Monte di Vico, seen from Villa Arbusto (cf. Fig. 5).

**Pl. 3.** Pithekoussai: the suburban industrial complex, Mezzavia. Detail of the Mazzola site (cf. Fig. 25).

Meanwhile, it may be observed that the above three sites, which clearly formed part of a larger whole, were all fully operational by 750; they are situated along an axis that is 1 km in length (Fig. 5); and, on present evidence, this was the greatest extent ever achieved by Pithekoussai.

Two vital features of Pithekoussan topography have not been excavated, nor need they be. The acropolis of Monte di Vico is flanked by a pair of perfect natural harbours: a narrow inlet to the north-west – the picturesque Baia di San Montano, backing on to the cemetery in the valley of the same name – and the broad sweep to the east that is now the bustling sea-front of modern Lacco Ameno. If, as is more than likely, recitations of the Homeric epics took place at Pithekoussai, the expatriate Euboean audience would surely have nodded approvingly at the practical advantage shared by their acropolis and (among other places) the tiny island of Asteris (Luce 1976), where Penelope's suitors laid in wait to ambush Telemachus on his return from sandy Pylos to Ithaca: 'In mid-sea is a rocky island between Ithaca and rugged Samos. Its name is Asteris; it is small, but it has two harbours with good anchorage' (*Odyssey* 4.845–7). For the commercial pursuits of the eighth-century Pithekoussans, 'good anchorage' was indispensable: and, now as then, the sea-front of Lacco Ameno is protected from all winds save those of the first quadrant – from which, on the other side of Monte di Vico, the Baia di San Montano affords more than adequate shelter.

It remains to note, finally, that the archaeological excavations have yielded geological proof that the physical configuration of Pithekoussai in the eighth century BC was virtually identical to that of Lacco Ameno in the twentieth century AD. Until comparatively recent times, it was thought that the eruption at Pithekoussai mentioned by Timaeus (Strabo 5.4.9: section 1, above) resulted in the creation of the Zaro promontory, which constitutes the far side of the Baia di San Montano (opposite Monte di Vico). Timaeus dates his eruption to a time shortly before his own, which would have meant that until some time in the fourth century the acropolis of Monte di Vico was flanked to the north-west not by a narrow inlet but by a broad curve like that to the east. The eruption in question was by any standards impressive: 100 million cubic metres of trachite were extruded and pushed almost 1 km out into the open sea.

Now, however, it is clear that Timaeus' eruption took place elsewhere on the island. The Zaro promontory was in existence long before the Euboean settlers began to bury their dead in the Valle di San Montano: they used blocks of unmistakably Zaro trachite to build tumuli over their cremation burials. And in the Mazzola area, the Apennine Bronze Age site that under-lies the eighth-century metal-working quarter was constructed on top of a layer of Zaro lava (Buchner 1986). In fact, the only real difference between the eighth-century and the modern lineaments of the Pithekoussai area is the result of the complex phenomenon known as bradysism (Buchner Niola 1965, 15), which affects the whole coastline of the Bay of Naples. There is good reason to believe that Ischia has sunk five or six metres into the sea since Roman times, and there seems to be no reason to doubt that the process began much earlier. For our present purposes, this means that in the eighth century the Baia di San Montano was correspondingly shallower and that both there and below the east flank of Monte di Vico there was more space than there is today for beaching boats. In the circumstances to which we now turn, this was probably just as well.

*Part two*

Pithekoussai in the second half of the eighth
century BC

# 4    Pithekoussai: the cemetery in the Valle di San Montano

No necropolis, however rich, can ever replace the living tradition of a nation.

(Momigliano 1963, 98)

## 1  The excavation

As we saw in the last chapter, the Pithekoussai cemetery occupies the Valle di San Montano, behind the natural harbour constituted by the bay of the same name (Fig. 5). Now, as in antiquity, the valley is delimited by the landward flank of the acropolis, Monte di Vico (Plate 2), and by a stretch of the lava ridge that turns into the Zaro promontory.

Although the alluvial material that overlies the Valle di San Montano has ensured that the cemetery was preserved virtually intact until proper scientific investigation was possible, it must be said at once that this is not an easy excavation. The valley is situated fairly and squarely in a thermal zone, which means that the temperature of the soil increases dramatically with the depth of the digging. The first, that is the latest, tombs encountered are more than 4 m below the level of the present ground surface; the last, that is the earliest, are between 3 and 4 m further down – where temperatures of up to 63° Celsius have been recorded. The effect of these natural circumstances on the contents of the graves poses many problems. Painted pottery in particular is sometimes found to have degenerated into a consistency resembling that of soft cheese; and delicate processes are required to lift it without increasing the already considerable hazards of subsequent cleaning, conservation and restoration – to say nothing of drawing, photography and cataloguing for publication. It is sad indeed that much of the earliest pottery and metal-work interred at Pithekoussai now preserves quite literally only a shadow of its original elegance. That anything remains at all represents a considerable practical achievement, involving years of patient and skilful work under far from ideal physical and administrative conditions. On the credit side, no thief or clandestine

excavator has ever shown any interest in such obviously unsaleable material.

The cemetery extends inland for at least 500 m; its width at the end
nearest the sea is approximately 150 m, narrowing to less than 75 m. The
roughly triangular area known to contain graves thus measures upwards of
50,000 m², and it was in continuous use for a thousand years, between the
eighth century BC and the third century AD. Two series of excavations have
taken place, between 1952 and 1961 and from 1965 onwards; they have
yielded around 1,300 graves of all periods from no more than 10% of the
cemetery's verified extent. The upper levels have produced late and relatively modest graves dating from the Roman period back to the fifth century BC; next come the seventh- and many more eighth-century cremations
under tumuli built of Zaro trachite blocks (Plate 4); and below these again,
a similar eighth- and seventh-century range of inhumations in trench
graves, amphoras (Plates 10 and 11) and other large pottery containers
originally intended for the transport or storage of liquids and other perishable goods; very few graves can be assigned to the sixth century. Within
the 'Euboean period', the transversal cut across the valley begun in 1965
has provided important evidence of chronological progress from early to
late towards the foot of the acropolis, and has in addition produced a
greater proportion of early Euboean graves than the first series of campaigns.

As already explained in the Preface, the definitive report on the 1952–61
excavations was completed in 1979 by the excavator of Pithekoussai, Giorgio Buchner, and the present writer. It was accepted in the same year for
publication as a *Monumenti Antichi* monograph at a time to be arranged
by the Editorial Committee of the Accademia Nazionale dei Lincei
in Rome; like the majority of our fellow workers in Italy, we naturally
hope that *Pithekoussai I* will appear in the near future. Since restoration of
the material from the second series of excavations is far from complete, it
should be noted that the information given throughout this chapter is based
on the findings of the first series (graves 1–723) unless otherwise stated.
Our picture of the first Western Greeks in death is thus based almost
exclusively on the 493 graves excavated at Pithekoussai between 1952 and
1961 that are conventionally and approximately dated to the half century
750–700 BC.

## 2    The burial rites

During the fifty or so years that make up the Euboean period at Pithekoussai, no fewer than five different burial rites were used (Fig. 6). They
occur in the following proportions:

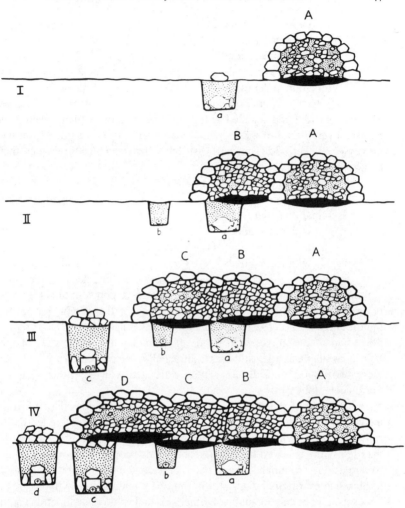

**Fig. 6.** Pithekoussai: the cemetery in the Valle di San Montano. Four phases in the development of an 'ideal' family plot (Buchner 1975, pl. 2).
**A–D:** cremations under stone tumuli (cf. Pl. 4). **a–d:** inhumations (**a,** baby in amphora; **b,** adult without grave goods in trench grave; **c–d:** children with grave goods in trench graves).

| | | |
|---|---|---|
| inhumation in trench graves, with grave goods | 39%: | 194 graves |
| inhumation in amphoras (*enchytrismoi*), with or without grave goods | 27%: | 131 graves |

inhumation in trench graves,
    without grave goods                16%:     81 graves
cremation under tumuli,
    with grave goods                  15%:     73 graves
cremation under tumuli,
    without grave goods               3%:     14 graves

The graves with goods yielded a total of 1,662 artefacts, which is well over half the overall total of 2,860 items catalogued in *Pithekoussai I* from the graves of all periods. They are distributed between the three rites that require their presence as follows:

inhumation in trench graves,
    with grave goods               71%:    1,180 objects
cremation under tumuli,
    with grave goods               24%:    402 objects
inhumation in amphoras (*enchytrismoi*),
    with grave goods    5%:    80 objects, in addition to the
                                            containers and their lids

On these figures, inhumation with or without grave goods in trench graves or in amphoras emerges as much more frequent than cremation under tumuli: there are 406 (82%) inhumation graves as against 87 (18%) cremations; and of the graves with goods the inhumations attract 76% of the objects available as against the 24% attracted by the cremations. Why? Can these two major ritual differences be correlated with any other feature? Fortunately, they can.

On the basis of skeleton length and of age determinations derived from teeth (Munz 1970), the following general rules – to which there are naturally exceptions – have been established: inhumation with grave goods is the rite usually reserved for children and young people (39% of the sample we are using); the amphoras and other large containers are invariably used to bury babies, often new- or still-born (27%); inhumations without grave goods usually belong to adults of either sex, and so do the cremations both with and without grave goods (34%). These percentages enable us to revise first impressions of relative significance based merely on a simple count of the two main rites: 406 inhumations and 87 cremations. We can now see that during the Euboean period the cemetery population at Pithekoussai was divided roughly into one-third adult and two-thirds pre-adult. Perhaps the most significant exceptions to these rules are constituted by the inhumations which apparently do not contain children, but which do contain grave goods; the latter are often very modest, which might lead us to suppose that the individuals concerned did not rank high in Pithekoussan society. This suggestion finds some measure of confirmation in the trench grave of a male whose teeth indicate that he died around the age of twenty. His grave goods included a fine set of iron tools, all suitable for woodworking, among them an axe, three chisels, two awls and a knife. For various reasons, however, it is not always possible to make a hard and fast distinction between 'juvenile' (the majority) and 'adult' (the minority) inhumations with grave goods. Even so, much can reasonably be deduced from even superficial analysis of the internal distribution of the grave goods between inhumations and cremations, and the results of one such analysis will be presented in the last section of this chapter. Meanwhile, the mechanics of the actual burial rites will be reviewed in greater detail in the remainder of this section; the arrangement of the graves in family plots will be demonstrated in section 3, and in section 4 the grave goods will be examined in their own right.

## Cremation with grave goods

The normal burial rite for Pithekoussan adults required cremation of the corpse and of the grave goods offered for burial with the burnt remains. Although a funeral pyre could no doubt be arranged virtually anywhere, it is more probable that a ceremony inevitably overlain with such profound religious and emotional significance will only have been carried out in one hallowed place: it is not yet known where the Pithekoussai *ustrinum* was. The fragmentary nature of many of the grave goods (especially the vases) and the even smaller size of the bone fragments suggests that, when its work was done, the pyre was beaten out very thoroughly – a most depressing thought for the modern restorer. Worse still, the objects retrieved from the cremation graves are usually incomplete: often no more than a third of a vase can be reconstructed from the sherds found. It seems clear that the charred remnants of the pyre, including the bone fragments and the shattered remains of the grave goods that had been burnt with the corpse, were gathered up and transported to the cemetery: some pieces would obviously be left behind, or even dropped on the way to the grave. On arrival at the appointed place, the residue of the pyre was deposited in a shallow and roughly circular scoop in the ground. For the excavator, the result of this part of the cremation ceremony is a lens of black earth containing a chaotic mixture of tiny potsherds, broken personal ornaments of bronze and other metals, pieces of bone and occasionally of carbonized wood. Either at this stage, or more probably at the pyre itself, any last smouldering embers were ritually extinguished by wine: in many cremation graves, the fragments of heavily burnt accessory vessels are associated with an almost intact and hardly burnt oinochoe (wine jug). Finally, the area of the deposition was delimited by a stone ring between 1.5 m and 4 m in diameter, which served as the base of a tumulus (1–1.5 m high) of Zaro trachite blocks.

There is nothing particularly aristocratic – or heroic – about Euboean society at Pithekoussai. Nevertheless, some key aspects of the cremation rite practised there by the prosperous middle class recall Homer's description of the funeral that Achilles arranged for Patroclus in the Achaean camp at Troy: 'First they extinguished the pyre with gleaming wine, all that the flames had reached, where the ash had fallen deep. Then with tears they gathered the white bones ... They marked out the circle for his grave-mound round the pyre, and fronted it with a groundwork of stones' (*Iliad* 23.250–6). Unlike those at Pithekoussai, Patroclus' funeral was held far from home and near the battlefield where the hero had been slain; the foundations of his grave-mound (or tumulus) were laid around the pyre, on which he had been accompanied by purpose-killed Trojans, sheep, oxen, horses and dogs, as well as 'two-handled jars [i.e. amphoras] of honey and oil, leaning against the bier'; and the ceremony was followed by funeral games on a scale that is unthinkable at Pithekoussai. But there is no reason to assume that the participants in the more modest ceremonies in the Valle di San Montano were unaware of the epic version of their ritual observances.

## Cremation without grave goods

In the sample that is being reviewed here, cremation is the rite that was used for 87 adults. Fourteen of them had no grave goods at all, a fact that renders their status especially difficult to assess. It may be significant that this is the only rite of the five identified in the Euboean period at Pithekoussai that is not so far attested in the later and poorer stages of the cemetery's use. For this reason alone, social inferiority or material poverty are not necessarily to be inferred. Giorgio Buchner has argued for a functional relationship between the empty tumuli, along with those that yielded only an unburnt or lightly burnt oinochoe, and another enigmatic feature that is characteristic of the cemetery's early history: large deposits of burnt sherds outside the graves, three of which were encountered in the portion of the cemetery covered by *Pithekoussai I*. Parallels for the complete absence of pottery from graves exist at both Eretria in Euboea and at the Euboean colony of Cumae on the Campanian mainland. The graves concerned at both centres are aristocratic; the deposits of burnt sherds at Pithekoussai consist mainly of high quality items that are not common in graves there. Among them are a number of kraters (bowls for mixing wine), a shape that is in itself indicative of a socially elevated lifestyle; one of them bears the painted scene known as the 'Pithekoussai Shipwreck' (Fig. 10), discussed in section 4 below. It could be that the fine pottery assigned to some 'upper-middle-class' Pithekoussan funerals was burnt on a separate pyre; then, in Dr Buchner's words, 'the remains of these secondary pyres were not deposed with those of the principal one. They were left to accumulate on the *ustrinum* until they finally became too inconvenient, when they were collected and dumped in a still unoccupied part of the necropolis' (Buchner 1982a, 285). In addition, Dr Buchner has convincingly likened the deposits of sporadic pottery at Pithekoussai to the *Opferrinen* ('offering trenches') identified by the excavators of the South Cemetery at the Kerameikos in Athens (Kurtz and Boardman 1971, 65f.). An Athenian analogy is not at all surprising, for the reason suggested at an early stage in the excavations at Pithekoussai: 'Eretria in Euboea may have caught the custom of cremation from Attica, and the Eretrians probably passed it on to Ischia in the West' (Webster 1958, 140). Certainly nothing is more likely than a substantial identity of belief and funerary observance at all levels of Euboean society at home and abroad in the eighth century.

Whether cremations under tumuli were marked at Pithekoussai is uncertain, but it would be odd if the last resting places of, say, fathers of families were not somehow identified. If they were, the markers have not survived in any recognizable form. It is possible that pottery vessels were employed, into which libations could be poured by interested parties on appropriate occasions. This suggestion is prompted by the fact that a few kraters had small holes bored into their base before firing; liquid offerings could thus percolate into the stem, and so into the tumulus below.

So much for the adults who were entitled to cremation: according to our sample, no more than 18% of the population (87 out of the 493 graves we are examining). The remaining 82% were inhumed in trench graves with or without goods, or in amphoras. Apart from a number of inhumations without grave goods, the majority of inhumations were children ranging from babies to adolescents.

*Inhumation in amphoras*

The 131 amphora burials (27%) of babies make up the second largest category of interments in our sample, a poignant comment on the high level of infant mortality throughout antiquity – and long afterwards: 'Nowhere in the world was a consistent mortality rate below one hundred per thousand even for infants (0–1 year) alone achieved until about 1900 A D' (I. Morris 1987, 62).

The containers used at Pithekoussai on these pathetic occasions were most frequently amphoras, local (Plate 10, right; Plate 11, right) or imported (Plate 10, left; Plate 11, left); coarse cooking pots (*chytrai*, as Plate 9, top) were sometimes used instead – the technical term often used to describe this rite is in fact '*enchytrismos*'. When the mouth of the container was too small to permit the insertion of the little corpse, the belly of the vase was broken; in some cases, it is clear that a trap-door was carefully sawn out. No attempt was made to seal the container securely: trap-doors were simply replaced; other apertures were covered, none too carefully, with large sherds from other amphoras; and the same is true of amphora mouths, although in a few cases these were loosely plugged or corked with stones or miniature vases. Lastly, the amphora was deposited, normally on its side, in a small trench. No evidence survives to indicate any degree of ceremonial observance: perhaps such frequent occurrences were regarded as purely family matters.

## Inhumation in trench graves

Older children and adolescents were inhumed in rectangular trench graves. In most cases, as at Eretria and Cumae, they and their grave goods were carefully laid out in a wooden coffin, the lid of which was usually weighed down with a few large stones – perhaps to prevent the ghost of the deceased from returning. Other stones seem to have been deliberately wedged between the coffin and the sides of the trench. Once the grave had been filled in with earth, its position was marked in some (possibly all) cases by a small pile of stones; full-scale stone tumuli, indistinguishable in outward appearance from those covering cremations, were erected over a very few rich inhumations.

As we have seen, the inhumations in trench graves without goods are frequently adult; generally speaking, the trenches in which they are found are shallower than the others, and none of them have so far yielded any trace either of a wooden coffin or of stone packing above or around the deposition. Sometimes the corpse has clearly been deposited on its side in a deliberately crouched attitude that is strangely reminiscent of indigenous funerary practice in prehistoric times (the Early Bronze Age burials at Gaudo near Salerno are a local case in point); this characteristic posture is never encountered among the inhumations with grave goods, which are invariably found in the supine position.

## 3   Family plots (Fig. 6)

The burial rites described in the previous section were all in use at Euboean Pithekoussai throughout the second half of the eighth century. In the nature of things, neither the choice of rite nor the precise place of interment can have been left to the uninformed or unaided preference of the surviving relatives: there were rules. It has become apparent that the cemetery con-

sists mainly of family plots. The principles involved are readily comprehensible, and are described in the following passage by the excavator of
Pithekoussai, Giorgio Buchner:

The key is provided by the tumuli erected over the cremation graves. The individual
tumuli are not isolated, but occur in clusters that are. In any given cluster, each
tumulus after the first was added to its predecessor in one of two ways. With the
first and more economical method, the base of the perimeter wall of the new
tumulus [Fig. 6, B] does not form a complete circle, but embraces part of the
preceding tumulus [A], which is thus partly covered and absorbed. In this way, the
black earth of the new tumulus [B] lies immediately adjacent to the exterior base of
the perimeter wall of the old one [A]. With the second method, a more or less
significant proportion of an existing tumulus [B] is actually demolished, and then
reconstructed within the next one [C], so that the new lens of black earth is either
immediately adjacent to the existing one [C-B] or partly superimposed over it
[D-C]. It is only rarely that a tumulus in a cluster is not connected to another in one
of these ways; even then, no tumulus is ever less than closely associated with the
others. Each cluster of deliberately connected graves evidently represents the successive depositions of members of a single family. It has been possible to excavate
only a part of some of the clusters that have been identified, but three (of which two
are in their turn connected, and should probably be considered as one) have been
excavated in their entirety. They each cover a strip of ground 14 m to 17 m long and
6 m to 10 m wide. No indication of any markers has survived; but they must surely
have existed, perhaps in the form of wooden stakes.

   Within the area of each family plot, the inhumation graves [a–d] of babies [a],
certain adults [b] and children [c–d] were prepared in the space not yet covered by
the tumuli. As the number of cremation graves increased, so the inhumation graves
were also covered by the tumuli. Each cluster thus provides a horizontal stratigraphy (particularly clear for the cremations) and a vertical stratigraphy of cremation graves over inhumation graves, which between them can tell us a great deal
about the relative chronology of the individual graves and their contents as well as
the demographic and social structure of Pithekoussai. (Buchner 1975, 70–1)

The funerary procedures described above by Dr Buchner confirm the existence of a significant degree of social organization at Pithekoussai in the
second half of the eighth century. This is a theme to which we shall return
in section 5 below. Family plots had to be assigned, used and maintained in
a manner that showed proper respect for the gods and for men.

   In circumstances at which we can only guess, it seems to have been
possible to dismantle early tumuli wholly or partly, and to superimpose a
new family plot on the remains of an old one. Incomplete stone rings have
been noted, and it is not unusual to find burnt fragments of *early* pottery in
the interstices of the stone tumuli of *later* tombs – a feature that is naturally
somewhat disturbing for an excavator. The most likely explanation is that
the lenses of black earth under the early, dismantled tumuli had been
carefully removed and scattered (a procedure that should not be confused

**Fig. 7.** Pithekoussai: the cemetery in the Valle di San Montano. Euboean krater
168–1 (Late Geometric II; associated with the inscribed kotyle and aryballoi,
Figs. 8, 9).

with the 'upper-middle-class' accumulations postulated in section 2
above). Accordingly, at Pithekoussai as elsewhere in the West, 'it may be
asked whether we are right to assume that the oldest graves found ...
belong to the period of the foundation' (Dunbabin 1948, 453). The possible
answers to this question have far-reaching implications.

## 4    The finds

The 1952–61 series of excavations in the Valle di San Montano cemetery
produced two individual pieces of the Euboean period that are justly

renowned in the annals of Mediterranean archaeology. Like the major categories described later in this section, both have attracted a considerable bibliography; with few exceptions, select reference to it is confined to the Notes on further reading, where the grave and serial numbers used in *Pithekoussai I* will also be found.

## *The Nestor kotyle*

At the time of writing, the single most famous find ever made at Pithekoussai is still the so-called 'Nestor Cup' (Fig. 8, no. 9): a kotyle (drinking cup) imported from Rhodes and deposited around 720 in the rich cremation grave of a boy aged about ten. It will be clear from section 2 that it is most unusual for such a young person to be honoured with this rite, normally reserved for adults. At some stage between its manufacture and deposition, the kotyle had been inscribed with three lines of verse (Fig. 9), of which the second and third are good epic hexameters: and since they are written by someone who used the alphabet of Chalcis in Euboea, it is quite possible that they were composed and incised at Pithekoussai. The verses seem to offer a playful challenge to the cup of wise old Nestor, the Homeric king of sandy Pylos:

**168**

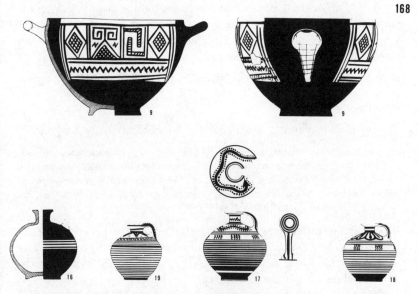

**Fig. 8.** Pithekoussai: the cemetery in the Valle di San Montano. Pottery from cremation 168 (Late Geometric II; associated with the krater Fig. 7): the inscribed Nestor kotyle 168–9 (for the inscription see Fig. 9) and the associated Early Protocorinthian globular aryballoi 168–16, –17,–18,–19.

**Fig. 9.** Pithekoussai: the cemetery in the Valle di San Montano. The retrograde metrical inscription on the kotyle 168–9 (Fig. 8).

Nestor had a fine drinking cup, but anyone who drinks from *this* cup will soon be struck with desire for fair-crowned Aphrodite.

Throughout the *Iliad*, Nestor was never less than generous with advice to his fellow Achaeans. Later, at home in Pylos, he was clearly delighted to perform the same service for Telemachus and Athena (disguised as Mentes, king of the Taphians) at an early stage in the quest for Odysseus (*Odyssey* 3.103–328). Greeting them on arrival,

he put in her hand the cup of sweet wine, and Athena rejoiced to find him so right in thought and deed, because it was to her first that he had offered the cup of gold. (*Odyssey* 3.51–53)

The cup itself may be the same one that is described in detail elsewhere:

Next a most beautiful cup, which the old man had brought from home – it was studded with rivets of gold, and there were four handles to it: on each handle a pair of golden doves was feeding, one on either side: and there were two supports below. Another man would strain to move it from the table when it was full, but Nestor, the old man, could lift it with ease. (*Iliad* 11.632–7)

It is tempting to attribute the verses inscribed on the pottery cup from Pithekoussai to a Euboean who wished to imply that the pleasures of love were preferable to the interminable good advice heralded by the appearance of Nestor's cup in the Homeric epics.

The kotyle which bears this humorous suggestion (if that is what it is) may be dated typologically and by its associations at Pithekoussai to the last quarter of the eighth century. The metrical inscription is thus one of the earliest examples of post-Mycenaean writing that have come down to us from anywhere in the Greek world. More significantly still, it is also the only piece of Greek poetry that has survived in its original form from the period in which it is usually supposed that the Homeric epics themselves were finally written down, at the end of a long tradition of oral poetry. As such, it affords a rare glimpse of the kind of usually invisible cultural cargo that the first Western Greeks brought to Italy, and eventually to ourselves. It is worth noting that the cheerful tone of the verses is highly inappropriate to their funerary context, and particularly so to the last resting place of a small boy. They are more redolent of the adult drinking parties, all male, known as *symposia*: and interestingly enough, the grave that contained the Nestor kotyle also yielded a set of pottery kraters for mixing wine (Fig. 7), a shape that is otherwise extremely rare in the Pithekoussan graves (though less so, as we saw in section 2, in the Pithekoussan equivalent of the Athenian *Opferrinen*). *Symposia* were convivial occasions, at which those present took it in turns to recite a none too serious poem. Since each poem had to be capped by the next member of the company, it is highly likely that a good many more verses remain to be discovered in the Valle di San Montano.

## The Pithekoussai Shipwreck

From poetry to painting. A locally made krater, roughly contemporary with the Nestor kotyle, bears a painted scene that depicts a shipwreck (Fig. 10). It is the oldest piece of figured painting ever found on Italian soil, and was reconstructed from fragments that were not found in a grave (see section 2 for the possible significance of this); the base of the bowl and the stem are missing.

The scene can best be read as a narrative. It begins with a capsized ship; the disaster has only just happened, for one of the steering oars is still in position below the curving stern. The sailors are swimming for their lives, but two of them are not quick enough: one appears to be dead, and is floating out of the scene at the extreme right; the head of the other is firmly locked between the jaws of an enormous fish. There is nothing to add, and the end of the story is signalled by the extraordinary device of a plump fish standing on its tail.

Some authorities have wished to see a connection between this scene and the legends relating to the homeward journeys (the *nostoi*) of the Homeric heroes from Troy: but it is not easy to identify the Pithekoussai shipwreck with the vicissitudes of any specific hero, and resemblances to Homeric shipwrecks are no more than general:

[Zeus] thundered and hurled his bolt into the ship; as the bolt struck, her whole frame rocked ... All the crew were swept overboard, and the waves tossed them up

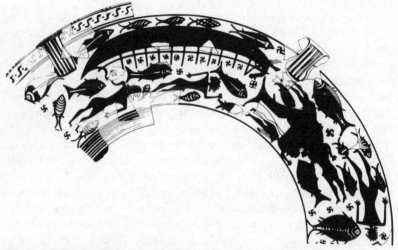

**Fig. 10.** Pithekoussai: the cemetery in the Valle di San Montano. The Pithekoussai Shipwreck: the narrative scene painted on the locally made Late Geometric krater Sp. 1/1, rebuilt from sporadic sherds.

and down round the ship like cormorants, for the god denied them their home-coming. (*Odyssey* 14.305–13).

Nevertheless, the Nestor kotyle has shown us that Homeric terms of reference are by no means out of place at Pithekoussai. And in those terms, the fate of those who died at sea was especially cruel: such unfortunates were denied all hope of being reunited with their fellows through proper burial. Clearly, this is particularly true of those who literally become 'food for the fishes' – precisely the horrendous process depicted on the Pithekoussai krater. It has been well shown that the scene effectively evokes the terrible consequences of death at sea described in two moving passages in *Iliad* 21 (Vermeule 1979, 184–5):

Now lie there among the fish ... Your mother will not lay you out on the bier and lament for you, but Skamandros will be your bearer, swirling you out into the broad lap of the sea. And fish rising through the swell will dart up under the dark ruffled surface to eat the white fat of Lykaon. (*Iliad* 21.122–7: Achilles taunts Lykaon, Priam's son)

I tell you, his strength will not save him, nor his beauty, nor that fine armour of his, which will lie somewhere at the very bottom of my flood covered deep in slime: and I shall wrap his body in sand, and pile an infinite wealth of silt over it, so the Achaeans will not know where they can gather his bones, such is the covering of mud I shall heap over him. Yes, and that will serve as his grave-mound, so there will be no need for the Achaeans to raise a barrow for his burial. (*Iliad* 21.316–23: Skamandros, river-god of Troy, threatens Achilles)

More prosaically, it may be recalled that nearby Cumae has 'the best fisheries for catching large fish' (Strabo 5.4.4), and that 'there *are* sharks in the Mediterranean' (Boardman 1980, 166). The Pithekoussai shipwreck krater may simply commemorate a tragic incident that brought a local trip or a longer haul to a sudden end. Such a possibility must always have been in the minds of constant navigators like the first Western Greeks; and it is likely that they were no less aware of the Homeric view of death at sea than they were of the epic version of their funerals. The appearance of the ship itself tells us little about its provenance. The sparse comparative material available from the Greek world of roughly the same period suggests that it is fairly close to Corinthian representations. This is perhaps slightly surprising at first sight, for Euboea was 'renowned for its ships' (*Homeric Hymn to Apollo* 219); but Euboea was also 'the further point of all' (*Odyssey* 7.321f.), and those of its inhabitants who were engaged in Western

**Fig. 11.** Pithekoussai: the cemetery in the Valle di San Montano. Painted decoration on the base of a local lekythos from grave 967 (Late Geometric I).

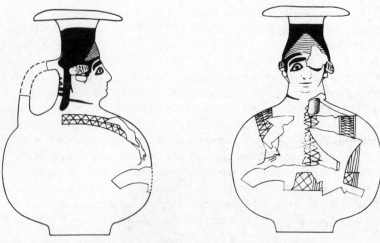

**Fig. 12.** Pithekoussai: the cemetery in the Valle di San Montano. North Syrian 'face aryballos' 215–4 (Late Geometric II; Buchner 1982b, fig. 2).

operations may have been able to avoid Cape Malea, the perilous south-east tip of the Peloponnese, by obtaining trans-Boeotian access to the Gulf of Corinth.

Three exceptional finds from the second series of excavations may be mentioned at this point: a fine amphora with a lion (or wolf?) on one side (Buchner 1971, 63, fig. 1); a local Euboean lekythos (slow-pouring jug for oil), with the typically Near Eastern motif – favoured by the great Euboean master, the Cesnola Painter himself (Coldstream 1971) – of a sacred tree flanked by a pair of rampant goats painted on the underside of its circular base (Fig. 11; Buchner 1971, 64, fig. 2); and a barrel vase depicting three women (the Fates?) carrying spindles (Buchner 1971, 64, fig. 3), which finds a close parallel for its unusual shape at Bisenzio in the hinterland of Southern Etruria (Åkerström 1943, pl. 12, 4). Like the Nestor kotyle and the shipwreck krater, these remarkable individual pieces suggest a notable degree of sophisticated contact between Pithekoussai and the outside world in the second half of the eighth century. The mass of less spectacular finds with which these pieces were found reinforces the impression on a grand scale.

## Pottery

The Nestor kotyle is by no means the only vase that reached Pithekoussai from Rhodes. Both the first and second series of excavations in the cemetery have produced scores of globular aryballoi (small unguent vases) of

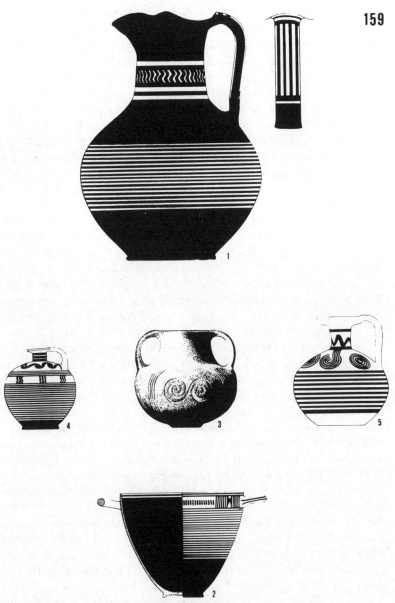

**Fig. 13.** Pithekoussai: the cemetery in the Valle di San Montano. Pottery from cremation 159 (Late Geometric II): local oinochoe 159–1; Early Protocorinthian kotyle 159–2; impasto '*anforetta*' 159–3, imported from South Etruria or Latium vetus; *Kreis– und Wellenbandstil* globular aryballos 159–5.

the '*Kreis- und Wellenband*' (circle and hook) or 'spaghetti' style (Fig. 13, no. 5; Plate 5, lower middle), a type almost certainly made not by native Rhodians but by Phoenicians living at Ialysos and bottling their unguents locally for export from around 725. No fewer than forty *Kreis- und Wellenband* aryballoi were found in an important new tomb discovered towards the end of the second series of excavations. It could be that the Nestor kotyle was brought to the West with a consignment of this attractive merchandise, and bartered to a prosperous Pithekoussan who had it inscribed. Aryballoi, or rather their sweet-smelling contents, were much in demand for funerary purposes. In addition to the semi-oriental variety from Rhodes, there are a few Levantine examples (Fig. 30) and a fine North Syrian specimen with the neck in the form of a woman's face (Fig. 12); it finds its closest parallels at Tarsus and at Zinjirli in Cilicia. Both cremations and inhumations have yielded numerous globular aryballoi imported from Corinth, where they are characteristic of the Early Protocorinthian stage (Fig. 8, nos. 16–19; Fig. 13, no. 4; Fig. 14, nos. 8–10, 12, 13; Plate 7, bottom right). In addition, C. W. Neeft has recently identified the work of three Corinthian expatriate potters/painters producing globular aryballoi in two Early Protocorinthian workshops at Pithekoussai. So far, their joint output stands at over thirty pieces, not only from Pithekoussai but also from Cumae and Suessula on the Campanian mainland, from Caere in Southern Etruria, and even from Bologna in the north. Clearly, 'immigrant potters were needed to supplement supplies' (Williams 1986, 296), and the clay of Ischia is plentiful and good. A good many local aryballoi were made by non-Corinthians at Pithekoussai (Fig. 14, no. 14), and it is not unusual to find aryballoi of more than one fabric in the same grave; local, Early Protocorinthian and *Kreis- und Wellenband* is a typical combination.

A similar range of fabrics is attested in the case of the lekythos, of which local (Fig. 11; Plate 8), Early Protocorinthian, *Kreis- und Wellenband* and Phoenician (Plate 5, right) forms have all been found, along with a further imported class of miniatures known conventionally as 'Argive Monochrome' (Plate 5, upper middle), but not necessarily to be connected too literally with Argos. The oinochoe is present mainly in a Greek-derived local form (Fig. 13, no. 1; Plate 5, left) with a number of fine imports from Corinth (Plate 7, left). Of the drinking cups, the Corinthian Late Geometric type of skyphos (with offset rim) named after the Sicilian site of Thapsos dominates the early years of Pithekoussai with both imported and locally imitated examples; the former typically have a 'window' or panel in the zone between the handles, the latter (Plate 6, top right) do not. The (rimless) kotyle sequence begins with imported and local (Plate 6, top left) versions of another Corinthian Late Geometric type named after the site of Aetos on Ithaca, where the English excavators first recognized the status of

**Fig. 14.** Pithekoussai: the cemetery in the Valle di San Montano. Pottery from cremation 152 (Late Geometric II): Early Protocorinthian kotylai 152–5, –6, –7; Early Protocorinthian globular aryballoi 152–8, –9, –10, –12, –13; large local aryballos 152–14.

no. 666 in their catalogue as the immediate predecessor of the Early Protocorinthian kotylai with thin walls – so thin, in most of the examples found
at Pithekoussai (Fig. 13, no. 2; Fig. 14, nos. 5–7; Plate 7, top right), that an
exclusively funerary function is surely indicated: 'egg-shell kotylai were
all right for the dead ... [but] your solid toper needed a more solid vessel'
(Benton 1953, 272).

Actual Euboean pottery has not so far been mentioned, and is in fact
comparatively rare in the cemetery: a few aryballoi; some interesting
Euboean imitations of Early Protocorinthian bird kotylai previously known
only from Euboea and Al Mina; and a few kraters, a form attested by
sporadic examples and in the rich cremation grave that contained the
Nestor kotyle (Fig. 7). But we must not forget that the locally made
aryballoi and lekythoi should also be considered as Euboean – made 'under
licence', so to speak, at Pithekoussai. Perception of this economically
significant phenomenon will be much clearer in future, following the pioneer application by A. Deriu of comparative Mössbauer analysis to a select
range of samples; it is now substantially possible to distinguish the physical
composition of painted Late Geometric pottery *made at* Pithekoussai from
that of similar pottery *imported to* Pithekoussai from the Euboean homeland. We also know that Euboean and Euboeanizing wares at Pithekoussai
share a firing temperature that was around 50° Celsius higher than that
estimated for the Corinthian samples analysed (Deriu et al. 1986).

The majority of the amphoras and other large vessels employed in the
*enchytrismos* rite are coarse local products (Plate 11) that seem to be
derived from Near Eastern prototypes – the 'Oriental ogival' form, also
present from an early stage. Other fabrics represented include the Attic
painted SOS type (Plate 10), imported and locally imitated, and other
specimens that have been attributed to Corinthian, Euboean, Chiot and
Phoenician fabrics. All of them reached Ischia as containers of oil or other
liquids such as wine: the random selection of 'empties' reused for burying
babies in the cemetery thus provides unusually direct evidence of what was
by any standards a complex trading pattern in the kind of perishable goods
that normally elude the techniques of archaeological retrieval. Wine and
probably oil were clearly being produced locally to fill the local amphoras
and to meet local needs. If any of it was exported, the identity of the
carriers is not easy to establish – and this is a problem that concerns the
imported amphoras, too. For example, there is no other Attic pottery in the
cemetery (or anywhere else at Pithekoussai) that is contemporary with the
Attic SOS amphoras, nor do we have any other reason to suppose that Attic
oil merchants distributed their own goods. The SOS amphoras at Pithekoussai might have been sent from Attica to the West via Euboean or
Corinthian intermediaries – or perhaps in the Phoenician merchantmen

who were most probably responsible for the contemporary appearance of the SOS type in southern Spain (Shefton 1982; ch. 5.3).

Amid so much pottery that is Greek, Near Eastern and local, two vases stand out as representative of a completely different cultural tradition. A miniature amphora of fine impasto with an incised double spiral on the belly between the handles is associated in a cremation tomb with Early Protocorinthian and *Kreis- und Wellenband* aryballoi (Fig. 13); another, in an earlier cremation grave from the second series of excavations, is associated with a Levantine aryballos (as Fig. 30) and a Corinthian Late Geometric Thapsos cup. Both *'anforette'* were produced on the Italian mainland, north of Campania, in South Etruria or Latium vetus: their presence and their exotic associations in the Valle di San Montano cemetery symbolize the function of Pithekoussai throughout the second half of the eighth century as a vital meeting place for East and West. The non-ceramic grave goods confirm this function in no uncertain fashion. From the East come literally hundreds of trinkets, many of them originally deposed in the *enchytrismos* burials of babies and in the trench graves of young children.

## Scarabs and seals

With the possible exception of Cumae, Pithekoussai has yielded the largest collection of paste scarabs of Egyptian type so far discovered in a Greek cemetery. The range includes some that have been defined as Levantine imitations, and the frequent occurrence of the class as a whole in the graves of babies and small children leaves us in no doubt as to the amuletic significance attributed to it by their parents.

Of particular interest is a scarab bearing the cartouche of the Egyptian pharaoh Bknrnf of Sais, more usually known by his Greek name Bocchoris, whose reign began around 720 and lasted until 715. In the latter year, he was besieged by Shabako, king of the Kushits, who let him die by burning. An alternative (and over optimistic) version of this episode, showing Bocchoris as the victor over the Kushits, appears on a vase of faience, also bearing Bocchoris' cartouche, from a tomb at Tarquinia in Southern Etruria. At Pithekoussai, meanwhile, very considerable importance must be attached to the appearance of an independently dated artefact in context: the dates of Bocchoris' short reign provide a secure *terminus post quem* for the deposition of the Early Protocorinthian aryballoi and other material associated with the scarab bearing his cartouche.

An apotropaic role may also be assigned to numerous scaraboid seals carved in red or green serpentine (Figs. 15 and 38). They belong to the North Syrian or Cilician type known as the Lyre-Player Group, after the motif on an example from Tarsus that led E. Porada to define the class in

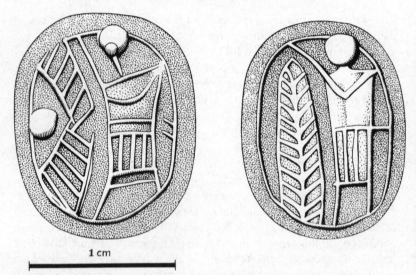

1 cm

**Fig. 15.** Pithekoussai: the cemetery in the Valle di San Montano. Lyre-Player Group seals 675–2 (*left*; Late Geometric I; Buchner and Boardman 1966, no. 3) and 284–15 (*right*; Late Geometric II (lower deposition); Buchner and Boardman 1966, no. 2). See also Fig. 38.

1956. In the Greek world, examples have been found at Aetos (Ithaca), Thebes, Delphi, Sunion, Aegina, Corinth, Sparta, Lefkandi (Euboea), Delos, Paros, Crete, Chios and at Lindos and Kameiros on Rhodes – a total of 61 seals in all, as against 36 from the first series of excavations in the Valle di San Montano (there are naturally many more from the second series); like the scarabs, the majority were found in children's graves. Pithekoussai has thus produced the greatest number of these attractive gems ever found at a single site. Elsewhere in Italy, one example from Cumae and four others from Etruria (Fig. 38, right) have been joined by a uniquely large specimen from Francavilla Marittima in Calabria; it bears five letters – another unique feature – that have been read as a signature incised by an Aramaic-speaking craftsman. Could the Calabrian specimen be the prototype for the Western series of Lyre-Player Group seals, especially those at Pithekoussai? We shall never know for certain. But it is interesting that a solitary askos of a Calabrian Iron Age type particularly common at Francavilla has been found in a grave at Pithekoussai. As luck would have it, this unusual item was associated with the Bocchoris scarab mentioned above – which thus transmits its chronological information to the South Italian mainland. Aramaic, incidentally, is the north-west Semitic language spoken at this time in the hinterland of Al Mina at the mouth of the Orontes, where a Euboean presence is attested from around 825 (ch. 2.3). The historical significance of a Semitic (Aramaic or Phoenician) inscription on an amphora from the Valle di San Montano will be discussed below (ch. 6.3; Fig. 29).

*Personal ornaments*

The indigenous side of Pithekoussai's complex and varied relationships with the outside world emerges from the typology of the many personal ornaments of iron, bronze, silver and electrum found in the graves of all rites. At this level – fibulas (Plate 9), arm-rings and pendants – the parallels with the contemporary Iron Age scene along the Tyrrhenian seaboard as far north as Etruria are striking indeed. As the struggle proceeds to establish which area was influencing the design of which fibulas in the other, it may be noted now that the Mazzola metal-working quarter has produced positive proof that fibula-making facilities were available at Pithekoussai itself (ch. 5.2; Fig. 26). And the clearly functional presence of so many indigenous types of personal ornaments has led Giorgio Buchner to the following conclusion:

> It cannot be supposed that the adoption of indigenous personal ornaments was a male idea, for the ornaments in question are mainly of female type; most of the men adopted only the serpentine bow fibula. It must have been the women themselves who insisted on wearing native ornaments: which suggests that most if not all the women at Pithekoussai were not Greeks, but natives who preferred the ornaments to which they were accustomed. (Buchner 1975, 79)

Before turning to the evidence yielded by the cemetery for the organization of what was clearly a complex society, we should look briefly at a seventh-century grave from the second series of excavations. Its contents show that although Pithekoussai was in decline after the end of the Euboean period, life (and of course death) still went on: a fine imported Middle Protocorinthian oinochoe decorated with fish, which deserves serious attention as a likely prototype of similar Italian products in the 'Cumano-Etruscan' class (so called for the reasons given in chapter 8); a bronze fish hook; some lead sinkers of a type still attached by fishermen in Lacco Ameno to their nets; and a fine set of Middle Protocorinthian ovoid aryballoi, one of which has a series of what look suspiciously like sea-horses on its shoulder (Fig. 16; Ridgway 1982a, 65–6, figs. 1, 2).

## 5  Social organization

In section 2, we distinguished five burial rites current at Pithekoussai during the Euboean period; three of them were seen to require the deposition of grave goods; and the occurrence of all five rites in family plots was

**Fig. 16.** Pithekoussai: the cemetery in the Valle di San Montano. Middle Protocorinthian oinochoe and ovoid aryballos from grave 1187.

demonstrated in section 3. Now that we have briefly reviewed the grave goods in their own right (section 4), the object of this fifth and final section of the chapter devoted to the Pithekoussai cemetery is to examine their distribution between the three burial rites that require them; and to assess the sociological evidence that thus emerges. As before, the information is derived from the 493 graves excavated between 1952 and 1961 that are conventionally and approximately dated to the half century 750–700. And before we go any further, we should examine the evidence for internal chronological division within this period.

In fact, two phases can be distinguished. They are conventionally known as Late Geometric I and II, and are dated approximately to the third (750–725) and fourth (725–700) quarters of the eighth century. The principal indicators of this division are ceramic. The Late Geometric II graves are characterized by a massive influx of imported globular aryballoi and thin-walled deep kotylai of Early Protocorinthian type, and the second Late Geometric phase at Pithekoussai thus takes its absolute dates from those applied to Early Protocorinthian elsewhere; indeed, as we have seen, Pithekoussai provides its own chronological information in the form of an Egyptian paste scarab bearing the cartouche of the pharaoh Bocchoris, whose brief reign (around 720–715) thus includes the *terminus post quem* for the deposition of the Early Protocorinthian globular aryballoi in the same grave. In Late Geometric I, such aryballoi as there are belong to the Levantine type; and imported Corinthian drinking cups are of the hemispherical and relatively thick-walled variety known as 'Aetos 666'. The validity of the division between Late Geometric I and II is also seen in the development of the most common local shape, the Greek-derived oinochoe. Examples from Late Geometric I graves invariably have a rolled handle, roughly circular in section, with solid paint on the back of the neck, leaving a panel at the front and sides (Plate 5, left); those from Late Geometric II graves have strap handles, rectangular in section, under which the neck-decoration is only briefly interrupted (Fig. 13, no. 1).

At this point, we are in a position to tabulate the distribution of the five burial rites and of the grave goods in the two periods (see Table 2). The figures are shown in percentage terms on Fig. 17. Fig. 17a shows a fundamental similarity in the proportions in which the five rites are represented among the 125 graves of Late Geometric I and the 368 graves of Late Geometric II; and Fig. 17b shows that the same is true of the distribution of

Table 2. *Distribution of burial rites and grave goods in Late Geometric I and II.*

| Rite | Late Geometric I | | Late Geometric II | | Total | |
|---|---|---|---|---|---|---|
| | Graves | Objects | Graves | Objects | Graves | Objects |
| Cremations with goods | 23 | 95 | 50 | 307 | 73 | 402 |
| Cremations without goods | 6 | – | 8 | – | 14 | – |
| Inhumations with goods | 60 | 279 | 134 | 901 | 194 | 1,180 |
| Inhumations without goods | 17 | – | 64 | – | 81 | – |
| *Enchytrismoi* | 19 | 8 | 112 | 72 | 131 | 80 |
| Total ( = 100% on Fig. 17) | 125 | 382 | 368 | 1,280 | 493 | 1,662 |

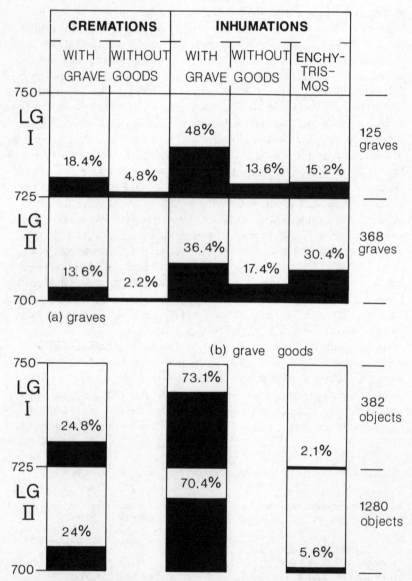

**Fig. 17.** Pithekoussai: the cemetery in the Valle di San Montano, 1952–61 excavations. Burial rites (see Fig. 6): distribution in percentage terms of **(a)** the 493 Late Geometric I and II graves and **(b)** their contents (1,662 artefacts).

the 1,662 objects (I, 382; II, 1,280) between the three rites that require them. No significance should be attached to the fact that Late Geometric II has roughly three times as many graves and objects as Late Geometric I: in the second series of excavations, the Late Geometric I period is represented by a larger number of graves in proportion to those of Late Geometric II.

It will be recalled that, on the basis of skeleton length and dental age determination, cremation graves may generally be identified as those of male and female adults, inhumations with grave goods generally belong to children, inhumations without grave goods contain adults (perhaps of inferior social class) and *enchytrismoi* are babies' graves. The social status of the smallest group, the cremations without grave goods, is tentatively defined as 'upper-middle-class'. In addition, the distinction between inhumations with and without grave goods is blurred by the existence of a certain number of inhumations with only a very few, or with 'working-class' grave goods. Their exegesis calls for value judgements concerning 'wealth', and will not be attempted here. In the matter of rank or class, the present writer sees no reason to contest a conclusion once reached by the doyens of modern mathematical archaeology: 'Division of graves into groups or classes purely by examination of a histogram of wealth scores (however devised) is more difficult than it appears ... Arguments for such divisions would have to be based on more evidence than a simple histogram of wealth scores' (Orton and Hodson 1981, 114). Nevertheless, Fig. 17b shows that in both Late Geometric I and Late Geometric II cremations attract just under 25% (I, 95/382; II, 307/1,280) of the available objects, while inhumations attract at least 70% (I, 279/382; II, 901/1,280). It seems reasonable to regard these proportions as systematic, and therefore worthy of further qualitative investigation.

This may suitably be conducted on the two largest categories of graves with goods, cremations under tumuli and inhumations in trench graves, and of the objects found in them: the 613 vases of fine potter's clay (I, 93; II, 520) and the 886 contemporary personal ornaments (I, 270; II, 616) which are found in the 73 cremations with grave goods (I, 23; II, 50) and the 194 inhumations with grave goods (I, 60; II, 134). The pottery may be divided into 'locally made' and 'imported', the personal ornaments into 'bronze and iron' and 'exotica'. Overall, that is in all three types of Late Geometric I and II graves with goods, these four crude divisions are represented in Table 3 (see also Fig. 18). It is, of course, dangerous to generalize from such a small sample. It may just be a statistical accident that in the sample we are using the proportion of fine imported pottery deposited (for whatever reason) in graves rises from just over 29% of all Late Geometric I fine pottery to just over 52% in Late Geometric II: the increase is partly (but not wholly) provoked by the massive influx of Early Protocorinthian and

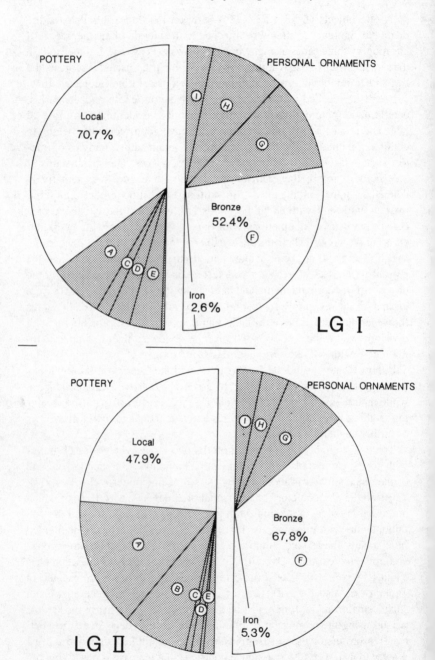

Table 3. *Proportion of grave goods in Late Geometric I and II.*

|  | Late Geometric | |
|---|---|---|
|  | I(%) | II(%) |
| Pottery |  |  |
| locally made | 70.7 | 47.9 |
| imported | 29.3 | 52.1 |
| Personal ornaments |  |  |
| bronze and iron | 55.0 | 73.1 |
| exotica | 45.0 | 26.9 |

*Kreis- und Wellenband* funerary pottery – especially globular aryballoi – in the later period. On the face of it, however, there is no such ready explanation for the contemporary *fall* in the proportion of exotica – Lyre-Player Group seals, Egyptian scarabs, various glass pastes, bone and above all precious metals (primarily silver) – from 45% of all Late Geometric I personal ornaments to barely 27% in Late Geometric II. With this in mind, we may now examine the relative proportions in which the Euboean and other inhabitants of Pithekoussai assigned vases of potter's clay and personal ornaments respectively to cremations and inhumations in the two phases under review. The distribution between the two rites of fine imported vases (categories A to E) and personal ornaments of bronze (F), silver (G) and seals and scarabs (combined in H) is summarized in Table 4. The incidence of cremation and inhumation graves containing these categories is set out in Table 5. Given that in both periods there are many more inhumations with grave goods than there are cremations, the figures in Tables 4 and 5 are expressed graphically in percentage terms on Figs. 19 (Late Geometric I) and 20 (Late Geometric II); comparisons can thus be made at a glance between the same rite in different periods and between different rites in the same period.

For the writer, the principal deduction that emerges from this somewhat laborious exercise is this: there is a clear 'preference' by cremations (adults) for personal ornaments of silver (G), and by inhumations (chil-

**Fig. 18.** Pithekoussai: the cemetery in the Valle di San Montano, 1952–61 excavations. Percentages of artefact categories represented in the Late Geometric I and II graves. The shaded areas indicate imported pottery (*left*) and personal ornaments (*right*). **A:** Corinthian. **B:** *Kreis– und Wellenband.*
**C:** Euboean. **D:** Argive Monochrome. **E:** Levantine. **F:** bronze and iron.
**G:** silver. **H:** scarabs and seals. **I:** gold, glass paste, bone etc.

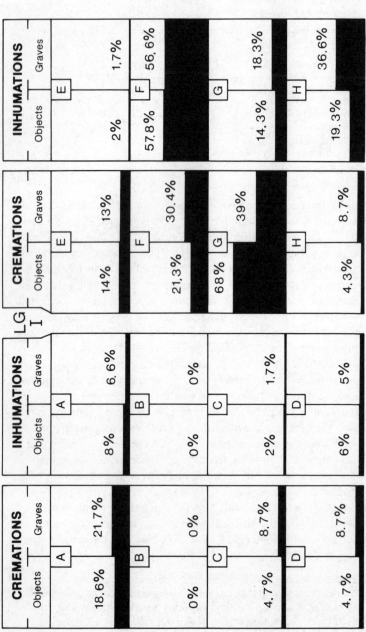

**Fig. 19.** Pithekoussai: the cemetery in the Valle di San Montano, 1952–61 excavations. Distribution in percentage terms of imported pottery and personal ornaments between the cremation and inhumation graves of the Late Geometric I phase.
**A:** Corinthian. **B:** *Kreis– und Wellenband*. **C:** Euboean. **D:** Argive Monochrome. **E:** Levantine. **F:** bronze. **G:** silver. **H:** scarabs and seals.

**CREMATIONS**

| Objects | Graves | |
|---|---|---|
| 18.6% | A | 21.7% |
| 0% | B | 0% |
| 4.7% | C | 8.7% |
| 4.7% | D | 8.7% |

**INHUMATIONS**

| Objects | Graves | |
|---|---|---|
| 8% | A | 6.6% |
| 0% | B | 0% |
| 2% | C | 1.7% |
| 6% | D | 5% |

LG I

**CREMATIONS**

| Objects | Graves | |
|---|---|---|
| 14% | E | 13% |
| 21.3% | F | 30.4% |
| 68% | G | 39% |
| 4.3% | H | 8.7% |

**INHUMATIONS**

| Objects | Graves | |
|---|---|---|
| 2% | E | 1.7% |
| 57.8% | F | 56.6% |
| 14.3% | G | 18.3% |
| 19.3% | H | 36.6% |

Table 4. *Distribution of objects by burial rite in Late Geometric I and II*

| | Late Geometric I | | Late Geometric II | |
|---|---|---|---|---|
| Objects | Cremations | Inhumations | Cremations | Inhumations |
| Vases of potter's clay | | | | |
| Total ( = 100% on Figs. 19, 20) | 43 | 50 | 172 | 348 |
| A   Corinthian | 8 | 4 | 53 | 105 |
| B   *Kreis– und Wellenband* | – | – | 28 | 54 |
| C   Euboean | 2 | 1 | 2 | 5 |
| D   Argive Monochrome | 2 | 3 | 2 | 5 |
| E   Levantine | 6 | 1 | 1 | 3 |
| Personal ornaments | | | | |
| Total ( = 100% on Figs. 19, 20) | 47 | 223 | 120 | 496 |
| F   of bronze | 10 | 129 | 50 | 364 |
| G   of silver | 32 | 32 | 62 | 43 |
| H   seals and scarabs | 2 | 43 | 4 | 35 |

Table 5. *Incidence of objects in graves in Late Geometric I and II*

| | Late Geometric I | | Late Geometric II | |
|---|---|---|---|---|
| Graves | Cremations | Inhumations | Cremations | Inhumations |
| Total ( = 100% on Figs. 19, 20) | 23 | 60 | 50 | 134 |
| With imported pottery | | | | |
| A   Corinthian | 5 | 4 | 24 | 49 |
| B   *Kreis- und Wellenband* | – | – | 10 | 24 |
| C   Euboean | 2 | 1 | 1 | 5 |
| D   Argive Monochrome | 2 | 3 | 2 | 5 |
| E   Levantine | 3 | 1 | 1 | 3 |
| With personal ornaments | | | | |
| F   of bronze | 7 | 34 | 23 | 91 |
| G   of silver | 9 | 11 | 20 | 17 |
| H   seals and scarabs | 2 | 22 | 4 | 28 |

dren) for personal ornaments of bronze (F). In human terms, this suggests
the existence of an age qualification for the personal display of precious
metal. Although the proportion of silver ornaments in the cremation repertoire of Late Geometric I is substantially higher than that of Late Geometric
II, the proportion of the actual cremation graves in which silver ornaments
occur remains virtually constant over the two chronological phases (I,
39%; II, 40%). On the imported pottery front, Corinthian (A) increases

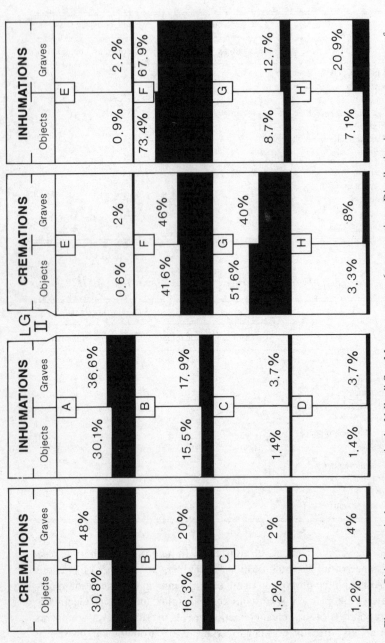

**Fig. 20.** Pithekoussai: the cemetery in the Valle di San Montano, 1952–61 excavations. Distribution in percentage terms of imported pottery and personal ornaments between the cremation and inhumation graves of the Late Geometric II phase. **A:** Corinthian. **B:** *Kreis– und Wellenband.* **C:** Euboean. **D:** Argive Monochrome. **E:** Levantine. **F:** bronze. **G:** silver. **H:** scarabs and seals.

greatly in Late Geometric II, when *Kreis- und Wellenband* (B) largely supplants the rarer imported fabrics – Euboean (C), Argive Monochrome (D) and Levantine (E); although they were not included in this exercise, it may be noted that around 10% of the amphoras employed in both periods for *enchytrismoi* are reused 'empties' from the Levant. The proportions of Late Geometric II cremations and inhumations in which *Kreis- und Wellenband* occurs are not very different (cremations, 20%; inhumations, 17.9%); for Corinthian, the gap narrows between Late Geometric I (cremations, 21.7%; inhumations, 6.6%) and II (cremations, 48%; inhumations, 36.6%). In both periods, a much larger proportion of Egyptian scarabs and Lyre-Player Group seals (H) are found with inhumations (children) than with cremations (adults), and in a larger proportion of Late Geometric I than of Late Geometric II graves: both phenomena were only to be expected.

More sophisticated sorting techniques might well bring to light repeated (and so perhaps significant) patterns at the level of grave and, more interestingly still, of family plot. Meanwhile, in the present state of the evidence from the cemetery in the Valle di San Montano, it seems clear enough that any social stratification there may be at Euboean Pithekoussai does not extend to an immediately apparent élite, like those which were developing at this time in Euboea itself (ch. 2.2) and on the Italian mainland (ch. 7.1). Political and military evolution at home and social change in Campania, Latium vetus and Southern Etruria are both worlds apart from the prosperous middle-class community in the eighth-century commercial and industrial centre on the island of Ischia, where arms and armour are so far conspicuous by their absence.

**Pl. 4.** Pithekoussai: the cemetery in the Valle di San Montano. Cremation tumuli during excavation (cf. Fig. 6).

**Pl. 5.** Pithekoussai: the cemetery in the Valle di San Montano. Pottery. *Left*: local oinochoe 490–1 (Late Geometric I; associated with the kotyle, Pl. 6, *top left*). *Top centre*: small Argive Monochrome conical lekythos 166–4 (Late Geometric I; associated with the Levantine aryballoi, Fig. 30). *Bottom centre*: *Kreis– und Wellenbandstil* globular aryballos 145–8 (Late Geometric II). *Right*: Phoenician lekythos 545–2 (Late Geometric II).

**Pl. 6.** Pithekoussai: the cemetery in the Valle di San Montano. Local pottery. *Top left*: imitation of Corinthian Late Geometric Aetos 666 kotyle type, 490–2 (Late Geometric I; associated with the oinochoe, Pl. 5, *left*). *Top right*: imitation of the Early Protocorinthian 'Thapsos cup' skyphos type, 498–2 (Late Geometric II). *Bottom left*: one-handled cup 310–2 (Late Geometric II). *Bottom right*: imitation of Early Protocorinthian kantharos, 622–3 (Late Geometric II).

**Pl. 7.** Pithekoussai: the cemetery in the Valle di San Montano. Imported Early Protocorinthian pottery from Late Geometric II graves. *Left and bottom right*: oinochoe and globular aryballoi, 359–1, –6, –7. *Top right*: kotyle 483–4.

**Pl. 8.** Pithekoussai: the cemetery in the Valle di San Montano. Local lekythoi from Late Geometric II graves. *Left*: 355–3. *Right*: 623–3.

**Pl. 9.** Pithekoussai: the cemetery in the Valle di San Montano. Cooking pot (*chytra*) and bronze fibulas from Late Geometric II graves. *Top*: 506*bis*–1. *Bottom*: 482–1, –2, –3.

**Pl. 10.** Pithekoussai: the cemetery in the Valle di San Montano. Painted 'SOS' amphoras from Late Geometric II *enchytrismos* graves. *Left*: Attic import, 398–1. *Right*: local imitation, 476–1.

**Pl. 11.** Pithekoussai: the cemetery in the Valle di San Montano. Coarse amphoras from Late Geometric II *enchytrismos* graves. *Left*: Oriental ogival type, 339–1. *Right*: common local type, 341–1.

# 5 Pithekoussai: the non-funerary sites

L'artisan est pourtant le héros de l'histoire grecque, mais c'est un héros secret.

(Austin and Vidal-Naquet 1972, 23)

## 1 The acropolis dump: Monte di Vico

*The site and the excavation*

As an acropolis, Monte di Vico (Plate 2) could hardly be bettered: it satisfies all the requirements of pioneers in a strange land. An inhabitable area of around 600 hectares is defended naturally by the slopes below, which fall steeply into the sea on three sides and into the cemetery in the Valle di San Montano on the fourth; the ancient settlement was convenient of access only by an easily defensible route followed now by the modern road which has been built up the east slope. The promontory lies between, and indeed dominates, two excellent natural landing places. The position of the Pithekoussai acropolis is thus similar to that of many other coastal settlements in the Greek world, and it also recalls the Phoenicians' preference for 'headlands and small offshore islands around the coast of Sicily, which they used as posts for trading with the natives' (Thucydides 6.2). The archaeological investigation of Monte di Vico has always been impeded by intense terrace cultivation of the vine, prior to which the soil cover was liable to erosion, especially at the higher levels; and it is in any case clear that the remains of the Greek town were plundered and destroyed from Roman times onwards.

As we saw in chapter 3.2, the presence of ancient potsherds and broken tiles on Monte di Vico was noted in the eighteenth century; these and other chance finds attracted the attention of authorities as illustrious as Julius Beloch and Paolo Orsi. Following the systematic collection of surface material from the thirties of the present century onwards, it was possible to deduce that the hill was occupied extensively in what was subsequently defined (on the basis of the cemetery excavation) as the Late Geometric II phase; sherds of the preceding phase, Late Geometric I, were also found over a wide area. The first and so far the last excavation on Monte di Vico was conducted in 1965, and is still unpublished save for brief preliminary accounts (see Notes on further reading). Its object was the investigation of a feature that had come to light during the construction of a large private villa on the east slope of the hill, overlooking the sea-front of modern Lacco Ameno. Here, a gully had been carved out of the soft rock by centuries of rain water running off the plateau above; the section under the proposed villa contained a vast quantity of ceramic and other material, deposited – whether by human or natural agency – in no sort of strati-graphical order. The sheer quantity of the material from the acropolis dump (known also, from the owner of the modern villa that led to its discovery, as the 'scarico Gosetti' or 'Gosetti dump') is remarkable; that it was clearly not in its original context when found is little short of maddening. There is, in fact, no evidence regarding the formation and status of the assemblage. Is it a true cross-section, and thus susceptible to interpretation by the standard techniques of statistical analysis? Or is it simply a random selec-

**Pl. 12.** Pithekoussai: the acropolis dump, Monte di Vico. Sherds of decorated impasto: Bronze Age Apennine Culture.

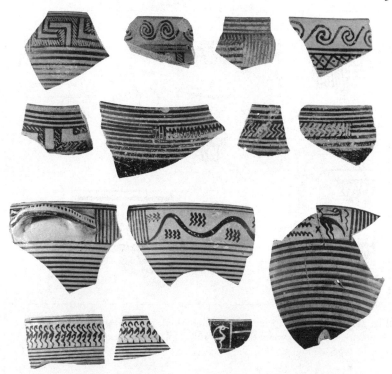

**Pl. 13.** Pithekoussai: the acropolis dump, Monte di Vico. Sherds of imported Corinthian pottery: Middle and Late Geometric, Early Protocorinthian.

tion, in which the strengths and weaknesses are dictated by purely casual – external and later – factors? In the absence of reliable answers to these questions, the material of the Euboean period from the acropolis dump on Monte di Vico can only be described typologically.

*The finds*

At least fifteen centuries are represented by the archaeological material recovered from the acropolis dump. The range extends from the handmade coarse pottery (Plate 12) of the native Apennine Culture of the Italian Middle Bronze Age (around 1600–1400) to the late Campanian black glaze ware of the second and early first centuries BC. Two notable lacunae must be noted at once: the absence of native pottery of the pre-Hellenic Iron Age and of imported Mycenaean pottery. These categories are lacking elsewhere at Pithekoussai, both in the excavations conducted to date on its

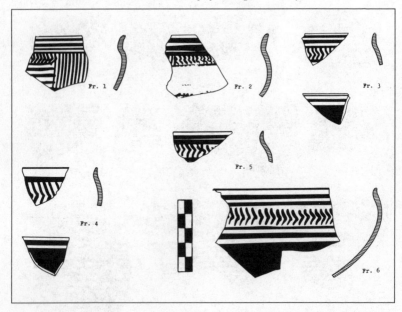

**Fig. 21.** Pithekoussai: the acropolis dump, Monte di Vico. Sherds of Middle Geometric chevron skyphoi (Ridgway 1981a, pl. 2). **1**: Corinthian. **2–6**: Euboean. For the type see Fig. 34.

component sites and in the systematic collections of surface sherds. On the evidence currently available, therefore, it would appear that the Euboeans chose to settle in an area that had no native population. This was by no means true of the island as a whole, as is indicated by the native village at Castiglione on the coast of Ischia between Porto d'Ischia and Casamicciola; the stratigraphical sequence there extends from the Bronze to the Iron Age, and a minute quantity of Mycenaean pottery has also been found. Vivara (the tiny island, now a nature reserve, between Ischia and Procida), Castiglione and Monte di Vico amount to a chain of what by any standards must be considered major sites of the Apennine Culture. The first two also attracted the attention of the Mycenaeans – impressively so in the case of Vivara (ch. 1.1); it is not clear why Monte di Vico should have been ignored – if it really was – by the Mycenaeans in the Bronze Age and by the natives in the Iron Age. On the credit side, fine painted wares of the eighth century, imported (Plate 13) and local, are present there in great abundance; material of the three succeeding centuries is scarce; and the Hellenistic and Roman period is relatively well represented. The chronological profile is roughly the same as that revealed so far by the cemetery; and Monte di Vico has also provided further evidence of Pithekoussai's survival, albeit on a much reduced scale, in the form of a fine series of painted architectural terracottas, some of them with the paint still well preserved, dating from the end of the seventh century to the fourth; they are closely comparable with the range, now available for study, from pre-Roman Pompeii on the Campanian mainland (De Caro 1986, 33–58 with pls. 15–30).

The acropolis dump has yielded the earliest evidence so far found at Pithekoussai for Euboean interest. Nine small fragments belong to Middle Geometric skyphoi with chevrons painted in the zone between the handles and with rims offset to varying degrees (Fig. 21). The fabric is clearly not local. One piece is Corinthian (Fig. 21, fr. 1; Plate 13, top row), and finds close parallels at Aetos (Ithaca), Corinth itself, Zagora (on the Cycladic island of Andros) and Old Smyrna; I prefer to define the fabric of the other eight (among them Fig. 21, frr. 2–6) as generically Euboean. In the Greek sequence, the chevron skyphos follows (but may overlap with) the type with pendent concentric semicircles (ch. 2.3; Fig. 4) and precedes the hemispherical Aetos 666 kotyle type, the development of which coincides with the transition from Middle to Late Geometric. The Late Geometric Aetos 666 kotyle makes its first appearance around 750; it stands – in substantial quantities – at the upper end of the local Pithekoussan sequence in the cemetery and in the industrial quarter of Mazzola (section 2 below), and is also present in the acropolis dump. There, however, the identification in 1981 of a minute quantity of imported Middle Geometric chevron skyphos sherds has at last provided at least some material that must necessarily be assigned to the period before 750. Examples of the same type have been found in native contexts on the mainland of Campania and in Southern Etruria (ch. 7.2; Fig. 34), where they are traditionally regarded as 'pre-colonial'. There is no reason to revise this definition simply because, for the first time, a few specimens have been found in a *Greek* context in the West: for the time being, it seems more prudent to allow Middle Geometric chevron skyphoi to retain their significance as trace-elements of activities preliminary to the establishment of a permanent base. Given the physical extent of Pithekoussai by 750 (Fig. 5), the diversification of its operations and not least the distribution on its component sites of imported and locally imitated (Plate 6, top left) Aetos 666 kotylai, these activities are likely to have taken some time – perhaps as much as a generation: Pithekoussai was not erected overnight, like a rural fair.

The discovery of an exiguous quantity of imported Middle Geometric pottery on the acropolis focusses attention on an unusual local piece from the cemetery: a skyphos that clearly imitates an original of the type represented by the single Corinthian fragment mentioned above. This interesting piece has been rebuilt from sporadic sherds: one fragment was found underneath a Late Geometric I grave, and the skyphos was almost certainly deposited originally in a grave that was subsequently dismantled. Was the potter who made it recalling the Corinthian model he had left behind in Greece, or had he been required to augment the supply of imported material?

In spite of the absence of any recognizable context, the nature of the eighth-century pottery from the acropolis dump complements the finds from the cemetery: as we should expect, there are certain basic differences between the funerary and non-funerary assemblages. Aryballoi, so frequent in the graves, are represented on the acropolis by a mere handful of fragments: the traditional definition of this shape as a 'perfume vase' should not deceive us into supposing that its function was even minimally relevant to the cosmetic demands of the living. Large Late Geometric kraters, local and imported (mainly from Corinth), are common; and many of them are decorated with motifs including men, horses (Fig. 27) and birds. As we saw in chapter 4.2, this shape is extremely rare in the cemetery; apart from the unique local shipwreck krater (ch. 4.4; Fig. 10), it was found (at least in the 1952–61 series of campaigns) only in the unusual grave that also yielded the Rhodian Late Geometric kotyle with an inscribed reference to Nestor and his cup (Figs. 7–9). Plates (Figs. 22, a-e), bowls and dishes are similarly rare in the cemetery and common on the acropolis, where, with the exception of a few Phoenician Red Slip examples (Fig. 31, lower), the vast

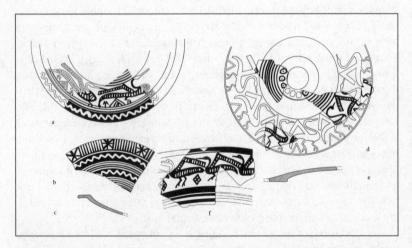

**Fig. 22.** Painted Late Geometric plates from Pithekoussai (**a–e**) and Eretria (**f**) (Buchner 1982b, fig. 13). **a–c:** from the acropolis dump, Monte di Vico (exterior, interior, profile). **d–e:** from the suburban industrial complex, Mezzavia (exterior, profile).

majority are of local manufacture. Cups are common in both the cemetery and the acropolis assemblages: in the latter case, however, thin-walled Early Protocorinthian kotylai are much rarer than they are in the graves, and thick-walled local and imported types of skyphos (notably Thapsos cups) and kotyle are much more common. Oinochoai, local and imported, are easily the most frequent shape both in the cemetery and on the acropolis. Excluding the large shapes (mainly kraters and amphoras), the principal activities suggested by a sample of approximately 10,000 painted sherds, local and imported, of the Euboean period are the following:

| | |
|---|---|
| pouring | 34% |
| (oinochoai and other jugs) | |
| drinking | 41% |
| (skyphoi, kotylai, kyathoi, kantharoi [as Plate 6, lower right], one-handled cups [as Plate 6, lower left], and other *poteria*) | |
| eating | 25% |
| (plates, bowls and dishes) | |

The principal fabrics represented in this sample are:

| | |
|---|---|
| Euboean | 3% |
| Corinthian | 16% |
| local | 81% |

It is noteworthy that the imported pieces are almost exclusively concerned with the consumption of drink rather than of food; this is also true of the other imported fabrics of the eighth and seventh centuries, present in relatively minute quantities (Argive Monochrome, Attic, Chiot, Cycladic, Etruscan bucchero), but not of the fine Phoenician Red Slip plates – which, as in the case of the 'Oriental ogival' amphoras in the cemetery, also inspired some competent local imitations (Plate 11). In addition, there are considerable quantities of coarse pottery: mainly locally made impasto *chytrai* (as Plate 9, top) and other kitchen shapes, interesting for their relationship with later Etruscan and Italic domestic wares.

Needless to say, the material from the acropolis dump includes some individual pieces of extreme interest. A fragment of a painted terracotta temple model of Geometric date is as yet the only one of its kind found in Magna Graecia; a female figure is depicted on the surviving door pillar. Another unique piece in the West is a fine example of Geometric seal cutting, preserved in the impression of the device on the neck of an unpainted amphora of uncertain non-local fabric (Fig. 23). Here, a man is shown carrying the clearly lifeless body of a gigantic companion on his shoulders. An impression from the same sealstone, one of a square class made in the Argolid and Cyclades, has long been known on a votive terracotta plaque from the sanctuary of Hera on the island of Samos. The scene depicted is that of Ajax bearing the body of Achilles to the Greek ships from the walls

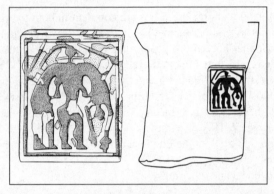

**Fig. 23.** Pithekoussai: the acropolis dump, Monte di Vico. Greek Geometric seal impression on the neck of an amphora: Ajax carrying the body of Achilles (Buchner 1966, 11).

of Troy. The Homeric connection is less direct than that indicated by the Nestor inscription from the cemetery, but hardly less instructive. The death of Achilles is described, not in the *Iliad* itself, but in one of the surviving poems of the Epic Cycle – designed at a later date to cover aspects of the Trojan adventure that are not mentioned in either the *Iliad* or the *Odyssey*. The Pithekoussai seal impression is virtually contemporary with the Nestor

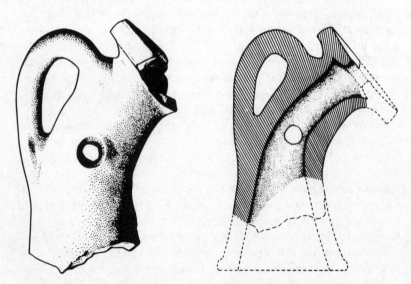

**Fig. 24.** Pithekoussai: the acropolis dump, Monte di Vico. Terracotta bellows mouthpiece (or pot prop? See *Notes on further reading*, ch. 5.1–2).

inscription, and suggests that allusions to Nestor's cup and Achilles' death were equally comprehensible in the last quarter of the eighth century.

It remains to mention a final major category of material from the acropolis, as unphotogenic as it is essential to the proper understanding of Pithekoussai's function: a substantial amount of iron slag, some terracotta *tuyères* (bellows mouthpieces: Fig. 24), the remains of two pottery crucibles (still encrusted with ferrous residue) and a piece of iron mineral. The discovery of this unlovely material in 1965 proved unequivocally that iron had been worked on an industrial scale at Pithekoussai. This had been postulated many times, even before proper excavation began; and the idea had been hotly contested by those who preferred to see a primarily agricultural basis for the foundation – an argument based on the later history of Magna Graecia rather than on the natural characteristics of the island of Ischia itself (ch. 3). The evidence for ironworking on the acropolis is devoid of anything remotely resembling an archaeologically datable context. The Pithekoussai *tuyères* find their closest parallels in late sixth-century Greek contexts at Marseilles and at Ampurias by the eastern Pyrenees; on the other hand, the cemetery in the Valle di San Montano had previously yielded a piece of iron slag in an unequivocally eighth-century context. Meanwhile, analysis of the piece of iron mineral from the acropolis dump has shown conclusively that it had been mined on Elba: indeed, the mineralogist responsible for the analysis was able to define it as pure haematite 'from one of the sources (notoriously exploited since antiquity) that make up the "Rio Mines," so-called because they are situated immediately above Rio Marina [on Elba's east coast].' (G. Marinelli, quoted by Buchner 1969, 97–8). With this remarkable discovery in mind, we turn now to an area of Pithekoussai that has provided further evidence for metal-working.

## 2 The suburban industrial complex: Mezzavia

### *The Mazzola site and the excavation*

The settlement of Euboean Pithekoussai was not confined to the promontory of Monte di Vico, but extended to the side of the Mezzavia hill (above the modern ring road) that faces the east flank of the acropolis across the modern town of Lacco Ameno (Fig. 5). Surface sherding suggested that the suburban complex took the form of separate nuclei in an area at least 500 m long; three such nuclei have been identified, all in operation by Late Geometric I times, and one was partly excavated between 1969 and 1971 in the area known as Mazzola, a natural amphitheatre enclosed by higher ground on either side. The metal-working quarter of Mazzola – with all that it

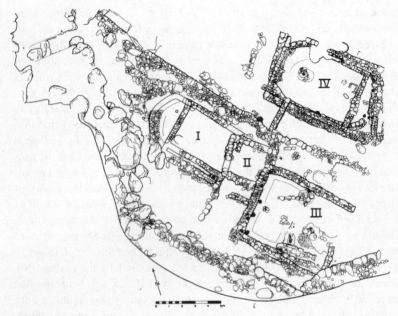

**Fig. 25.** Pithekoussai: the suburban industrial complex, Mezzavia. Plan of the Mazzola site (Buchner 1971, fig. 5) (cf. Pl. 3).

implies for Pithekoussai's *raison d'être* – owes its preservation and excavation to its position: its peripheral location is precisely what we should expect, for early smiths needed to be near the sources of the charcoal that they used in vast quantities, and their fellow citizens were doubtless anxious to avoid the risk of fires and the certainty of malodorous smoke in the main settlement.

The investigation yielded the remains of a structural complex (Plate 3; Fig. 25) that can be dated by its ceramic finds to the period between the middle of the eighth and the beginning of the seventh centuries. It is thus contemporary with the period that we have examined in the cemetery and on the acropolis. Desertion of the site during the first quarter of the seventh century seems to have been complete, save for the reoccupation of a limited area in the first half of the sixth century that is indicated by the walls of a structure made of squared blocks of green Epomeo tufa. In sharp contrast, the walls of the earlier period are made of pieces of local Zaro trachite with earth in the interstices; they are well preserved and have not been artificially disturbed since occupation ceased, save by the superficial damage caused by the terracing and vine growing of relatively recent times.

Of the four structures shown on Fig. 25, only the apsidal building 1 seems to have been intended for living in: a large rectangular room and a smaller room with a curving external wall at the north-west end. This is also the only building that shows no sign of reconstruction; fragments of virtually complete vases (including a fine painted Geometric krater) on the floor, in which was embedded a whole cooking pot of coarse pottery, speak for sudden abandonment following destruction, provisionally dated by J. J. Klein to around 720. Perhaps it is not too fanciful to recall that Strabo specified earthquakes as one of the alarming natural phenomena that drove the Euboeans away from Pithekoussai (ch. 3.1). In the western part of the Mazzola area, seismic activity would soon have brought massive boulders crashing down from the Mezzavia ridge. The other structures were all concerned in one way or another with metal-working. The two successive floor levels of Structure III yielded many pieces of bloom and iron slag, and the floor surfaces were impregnated with tiny iron fragments. This was surely a blacksmith's workshop, a diagnosis that receives considerable support from the heavily burnt area – which may reasonably be identified as a forge – in the adjoining open courtyard. At some stage in the Euboean period, the originally oval Structure IV was adapted to make a rectangular building; inside, a rectangular arrangement of heavily burnt mud bricks seems to be another forge, near which were found two large flat polished pieces of hard phonolith that could well have been used as anvils.

## The finds

The material found at Mazzola confirms in full that metal was extensively worked at Pithekoussai in the second half of the eighth century. As we saw in section 1, the only previous evidence for the existence of this activity at such an early date was the discovery of a piece of iron slag in an unequivocally eighth-century context in the cemetery; the substantial quantities of the same material, the piece of pure Elban haematite, the crucibles and the *tuyères* from the acropolis dump are all devoid of chronological context. In view of the sixth-century date of the best parallels for the *tuyères* from Monte di Vico, it could in fact be that metal-working for local purposes was transferred to Monte di Vico after the abandonment of the Mazzola site. There, it is clear that iron was not the only metal that was being worked. The detritus that accumulated outside Structure IV included numerous snippets of bronze sheet and wire, a small bronze ingot, drops of greenish vitreous slag and pieces of lead. Among this foundry refuse, an unfinished fibula, obviously discarded during production as defective (Fig. 26, top), shows conclusively that the eighth-century community at Pithekoussai was capable of manufacturing its own personal ornaments of bronze. Further

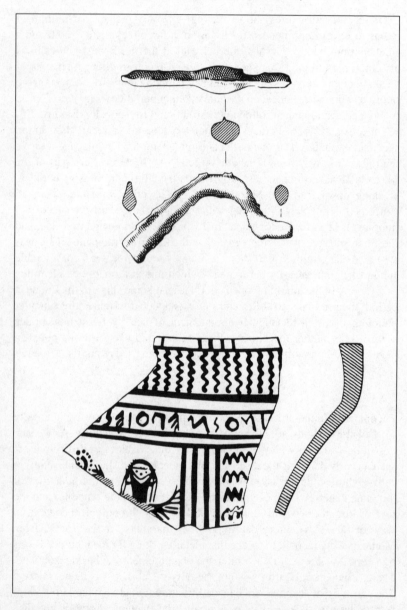

**Fig. 26.** Pithekoussai: the suburban industrial complex, Mezzavia. Small finds (Buchner 1971, figs. 7, 8). *Top*: bronze fibula, discarded during production (note casting seams). *Bottom*: rim-sherd of a local Late Geometric krater, with painted retrograde inscription . . . *inos m'epoies[e]* ('[a potter whose name ends in]–inos made me') – the earliest known example of this well-known formula.

proof is provided by a few pieces of bone from which had been sawn elements suitable for attachment to fibulas of the type – especially common in the eighth-century graves in the cemetery (Plate 9, lower pair) – which has bone and amber on its bow.

From the surface of the rubbish dump against the north-west wall of Structure IV comes another unusual small find: a disc of lead bound in a bronze ring. It weighs 8·79 g, which is extremely close to the standard weight – 8·72 g – of the Euboic-Attic stater. Hitherto, it has been supposed that this standard reached the West early in the fifth century, when the Hellenized Sicel towns began to strike small silver coins (*litrae*) of 0·87 g, one-tenth of the Euboic-Attic stater. From Sicily, the Euboic-Syracusan *litra* of 0·87 g subsequently passed to Etruria as the basis of two of the four standards on which silver coins were struck (Hill 1899). In both Sicily and Etruria, the unit of the silver coins (0·87 g) was fifteen times as heavy as the contemporary unit of the gold ones (0·058 g). There can be little doubt that the bronze-bound lead disc from Mazzola is a weight, in use most probably not later than the date of the latest diagnostic pottery in the rubbish dump in which it was found – the first quarter of the seventh century: it is unlikely, but technically not impossible, that the piece had slipped into the early context in which it was found from the dump of the sixth-century reoccupation period superimposed directly above it. Discarding this remote possibility, we are left with the virtual certainty that the Euboean standard was being employed in the West a good two centuries before its use had previously been suspected. It is on all counts likely that the Mazzola pre-monetary weight was used either to weigh out quantities of precious metal – such as that required for the manufacture of the many silver personal ornaments in the eighth-century graves – or, perhaps as part of a set, to weigh the finished products with a view to establishing their value. Jewellers' workshops at Pithekoussai, where silver and gold could be worked, are thus a real possibility – the archaeological demonstration of which has led to the better understanding of Strabo's reference to *chruseia/chrusia* as a feature of the Euboeans' prosperity in their first Western establishment (ch. 3.1).

Substantial quantities of pottery have been found at the Mazzola site, mostly fragmentary, and characterized by the disturbingly frequent phenomenon of joins between sherds from widely separated parts of the excavation. In fact, the presence of pottery does not seem to have been directly occasioned by the most obvious function of the buildings in which it was found. Mixed with earth, it seems rather to have served to raise the levels of the floors in the successive periods of the half century or so that the workshops were in use. As in the Monte di Vico assemblage, funerary shapes (such as aryballoi) are virtually absent from Mazzola, while domestic forms (such as large painted and frequently figured kraters and amphoras) are common. The imported wares, though far from undistinguished, add little to the range represented in the cemetery and on the acropolis; an unusual piece is a fragment of a Rhodian Late Geometric kotyle of the same type as the inscribed example in the cemetery. Typologically, the earliest Greek shape is that represented by a number of locally made kotylai (as Plate 6, left) that imitate the Corinthian Late Geometric Aetos 666 variety: this implies that the Mazzola workshops were instituted slightly later than the stage attested by the Middle Geometric chevron skyphoi on the acropolis – which is only to be expected. Other similarities between the Monte di Vico and Mazzola assemblages include evidence for previous Apennine Bronze Age habitation and the absence both of Mycenaean contacts and of local pre-Hellenic Iron Age material.

One ceramic find bears unusually explicit witness to an industrial activity that was almost certainly not carried out at Mazzola: potting. A small rim-and-shoulder fragment from a local krater (Fig. 26, lower), found under one of the foundation stones of Structure II, bears the following painted retrograde inscription: '... *inos m'epoiese*' ('... inos made me'), a potter's, signature of the late eighth century, and thus the earliest occurrence of this well-known formula ever found anywhere in the Greek world. Sadly, the name is incomplete, and so is the curious winged creature depicted; it may be a sphinx, and is in any case clearly oriental in appearance.

## 3   Conclusions

### *Pottery*

Although neither of them were found in their original contexts, the ceramic assemblages of Monte di Vico and Mazzola have between them greatly expanded the essentially funerary image of the pottery in use at Pithekoussai during the second half of the eighth century. A whole new class of painted pottery has emerged; it is clearly local, and its birth may safely be assigned to the Late Geometric I period defined in the cemetery – where, as in the early graves of colonial Cumae, it is represented by aryballoi and lekythoi appropriate to the funerary context. At Cumae, many of these distinctive small funerary vases were initially defined as Cretan by H. Payne (1931, 4 n. 2), a diagnosis generally accepted until Giorgio Buchner discussed the many more examples of the same class from his excavations in the Valle di San Montano. He suggested that Payne's Cretan definition be revised to Euboean (Buchner 1964, 268f., followed by Coldstream 1968a, 194f.), and later added the vital qualification 'Made in Ischia' (Buchner 1971, 67).

The products of the expatriate Euboean potters encountered on the non-funerary sites at Pithekoussai were influenced, directly or indirectly, by the contemporary styles of Corinth and Athens; but this eclectic tendency, perceptible also at home in Euboea, did not prevent the flowering of highly individual and occasionally wayward local talent. A detailed analysis of the Pithekoussai Geometric style is out of place prior to full publication of the material from both the funerary and non-funerary sites; suffice it to say here that the majority of its component features, both figured and purely decorative, will be found on the magnificent Late Geometric krater by the Cesnola Painter, assigned to Euboea by J. N. Coldstream (1971). The only

**Fig. 27.** Pithekoussai: panel depicting a horse tied to a manger with a double axe suspended above. Reconstructed from numerous sherds of Late Geometric kraters from the non-funerary sites, Monte di Vico and Mezzavia.

common Pithekoussan motif which does not occur on the Cesnola krater is a strange construct comprising a hatched upright triangle surmounted by a hatched horizontal bar with downward pointing terminals at right angles. Whatever the affinities of this ungainly item, it was clearly of some importance: it is a constant feature of the panels on local kraters that depict a horse tied to a manger with a double axe suspended above (Fig. 27). These panels are often found in pairs, with the horses facing each other. Whether or not they should be connected with the *Hippobotai*, the horse-raising aristocracy of Euboea (Strabo 10.1.8), it is probable that a certain degree of nostalgia for the rolling grassy uplands of home was involved. Meanwhile, as we shall see in the final part of this book, the manufacture and painting of vases were by no means the least of the services that the Euboeans had to offer the native élites of the mainland after the demise of Pithekoussai at the end of the eighth century.

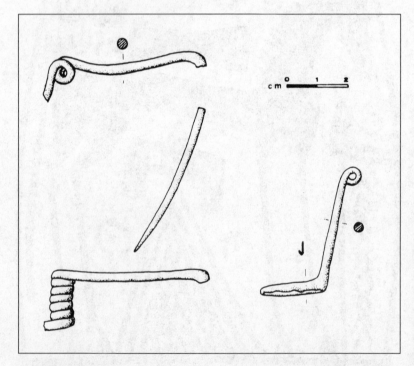

**Fig. 28.** Bronze fibulas of the Iberian type '*a doble resorte*' (Lo Schiavo 1978, fig. 7). *Left*: from Pithekoussai, fill of grave 700 (probably Late Geometric II) in the Valle di San Montano cemetery. *Right*: from the Grotta Pirosu, Su Benatzu (Santadi, Cagliari province) in Sardinia.

*Metallurgy*

Silver and gold do not occur naturally on Ischia: their existence on the island has long been recognized as geologically impossible (Pais 1908b, 184). The sources on which the Mazzola jewellers might have drawn are not infinite. Early Euboean interest in southern Illyria, rich in silver, is mentioned in the ancient sources (Strabo 10.1.15; Pausanias 5.22.3–4) but – perhaps not surprisingly (Bakhuizen 1976, 25) – so far not demonstrated by archaeology. Sardinia is another possibility and has the advantage of being relatively close to Ischia (Ridgway 1986; Lo Schiavo and Ridgway 1987); a certain degree of contact is already demonstrated by a Euboeanizing painted urn, accepted by Buchner as a Pithekoussan product, from the Phoenician *tophet* at Sulcis, south-west of Cagliari, and by the fact that an Iberian fibula from the same general area finds its only parallel in Italy at Pithekoussai (Fig. 28). Further afield, there are parallels at Pithekoussai for the Oriental material found in the excavation of the remains of a Phoenician or Phoenicianizing community of silver miners at Rio Tinto in Spain (Blanco and Luzón 1969). In this connection, B. B. Shefton has discussed a fascinating passage in the undatable (but post-Aristotelian) author of a late tract which contains a variety of early information concerning the Far West:

> It is said that those of the Phoenicians who first sailed to Tartessus, after importing to that place oil, and other small wares of maritime commerce, obtained for their return cargo so great a quantity of silver, that they were no longer able to keep or receive it, but were forced when sailing away from those parts, to make of silver not only all the other articles which they used, but also all their anchors. (*De mirabilibus auscultationibus* 135, trans. L. D. Dowdall; quoted by Shefton 1982, 341)

So far, no silver anchors of Phoenician type have been found at Pithekoussai. But a number of Attic SOS amphoras, suitable for transporting oil and similar to those found at Pithekoussai (Plate 10, left), have been found in Spain. Shefton has argued brilliantly for their carriage by Phoenician merchantmen, noting inter alia the similarity in the Greek (including Pithekoussan) distribution of this type and of the *Kreis- und Wellenbandstil* aryballoi, probably made at Ialysos on Rhodes by Phoenician entrepreneurs (ch. 4.4). It remains true that if the Pithekoussan silversmiths were dependent on Phoenician suppliers operating out of Sardinia or Spain, or even if some of the silversmiths were themselves Phoenician, they seem to have been working to the Euboean standard suggested by the Mazzola weight.

Like silver and gold, neither iron nor the constituent elements of bronze (copper and tin) have ever been naturally available anywhere on Ischia: they all had to be brought there to be worked. The most likely source for the base metals is indicated by the analysis of the piece of iron mineral from the acropolis dump on Monte di Vico: the island of Elba and the *Colline metallifere* (the mineral-rich zone of north-west Tuscany) in general. A staggering amount of human labour was inevitably required to transport heavy raw material from the area of, say, Populonia on the coast of Etruria or Rio Marina on Elba to the Mezzavia ridge above modern Lacco Ameno on Ischia – and to do so on the regular basis that alone would make the operation worthwhile. More hard work was required to cut down the trees necessary, on an enormous scale, to feed the furnaces. Not much of this is conveyed by Hesiod's elegant (and contemporary) metaphorical reference to 'iron melting in glowing mountain fires' (*Theogony* 865). Those actually involved would more probably have been better pleased by a prosaic account of the similar processes carried out many centuries later by their Roman successors in the same area:

This island [Aithaleia = Elba] possesses a great quantity of iron mineral, which they mine for smelting and working to extract the metal ... Those employed in this work split the rock and burn the separate chunks in certain ingenious furnaces, obtaining medium-sized lumps similar in appearance to sponges. These are sold or bartered to merchants, who take them to Dicearcheia [Roman Puteoli = modern Pozzuoli, south of Cumae on the Campanian mainland], or to some other commercial centre, where there are people who buy them so that their armies of metal-workers can refine them further and turn them into all kinds of artefacts. (Diodorus Siculus 5.13)

## *Incognita*

In the previous chapter, and in the first two sections of this one, I have briefly described those areas where archaeology has retrieved evidence for eighth-century occupation at Pithekoussai: the cemetery, the acropolis and the workshops. Of these, the first and second provide ample proof for the hypothesis that Pithekoussai's importance depended on its status as the Western headquarters of a far-flung network of Euboean trade; the third demonstrates that Pithekoussai was an industrial as well as a commercial centre. The picture that emerges is necessarily incomplete, however, not only because full publication of the excavations has not yet been achieved, but also because even the massive quantities of material yielded by the three sites described constitute no more than the tip of the iceberg – compared with what has been lost over the centuries, and with what is still concealed beneath the soil. Of the cemetery in the Valle di San Montano, only a fraction has been excavated; of the acropolis, Monte di Vico, our only source of knowledge is a dump; of the industrial complex at the foot of the Mezzavia ridge, one out of three (or more) nuclei of workshops has been partly excavated.

We have no evidence whatsoever concerning the infrastructure – warehouses, for example – that was obviously required by the activities of a busy trading port. Such necessary features were most probably situated along the eastern dock side, the broad sweep that is now the bustling sea-front of modern Lacco Ameno. And although extensive harbour works were probably not required, the shipwreck krater should remind us that shipyards were indispensable for construction and maintenance. In spite of the many varieties of imported pottery, locally produced wares are by far the most common on all three sites: so far, there is no trace of a single potter's workshop, let alone the true potters' quarter that presumably contained the local and expatriate specialists. The Pithekoussan *kerameikos* was most probably situated in the general area of the modern Piazza di Santa Restituta, where there was once a supply of the fresh water needed to wash and work the clay; nearby, under the present Basilica di Santa Restituta (Ischia's patron saint), the researches of Don Pietro Monti (1980, 137–49) have revealed impressive remains of Hellenistic and Roman kilns.

## 4  Demography

Finally, it is not easy to estimate the actual population of Pithekoussai at any stage in the fifty years or so of its Euboean period. Inevitably, such evidence as there is on this subject comes from the cemetery. The 493 graves considered in chapter 4 were excavated in an area that amounts to not less than 2·5% and not more than 5% of the whole cemetery. The total number of depositions made in the Valle di San Montano between 750 and 700 could thus lie between a minimum of 9,860 and a maximum of 19,720, identified by the five rites discussed in chapter 4.2 as follows:

|  |  | minimum | maximum |
|---|---|---|---|
| 'upper(?) middle-class' adults | ( 3%) | 296 | 592 |
| 'middle-class' adults | (15%) | 1,479 | 2,958 |
| 'other' adults | (16%) | 1,578 | 3,156 |
| new- or still-born babies | (27%) | 2,662 | 5,324 |
| mainly children or young persons | (39%) | 3,845 | 7,690 |

These total figures yield an average of between 197 and 394 interments in each of the fifty years involved; between 35 and 70 would have been adult cremations (18%) – perhaps one funeral a week for most of the year; between 53 and 106 would have been *enchytrismos* burials of babies (27%) – one or two a week.

What is the relationship between the cemetery population and the resident living population? An annual death rate of 30 per 1,000 has been suggested as the norm for agricultural societies in which a full age structure is represented (I. Morris 1987, 74). In view of what may be an unusually high proportion of *enchytrismoi* in the Pithekoussai cemetery (though not of infant deaths in the settlement: I. Morris 1987, 61–2), it seems advisable *either* (i) to discount this category (27%) altogether, on the grounds that its members did not survive for long enough to take their place in society, *or* (ii) to raise the overall death rate from 30 to 40 per 1,000. The 'burying group' or living population thus emerges in round figures as not less than 4,800 (i) or 4,930 (ii) and not more than 9,600 (i) or 9,860 (ii) at any time between 750 and 700. These figures are reached by the formula

$$p = \frac{1,000}{(dt/n)} \text{ (I. Morris 1987, 74)},$$

where $p$ stands for the population of the burying group, $d$ the death rate per 1,000 (here 30 (i) or 40 (ii)), $t$ the time span in years (here 50) and $n$ the number of burials made (here 7,198 – 14,396 (i) or 9,860 – 19,720 (ii)). If method (i) is followed, the percentage of adults rating cremation with or without grave goods under tumuli must be adjusted to 24·66% to allow for the elimination of the *enchytrismoi* from the overall burial totals; on method (ii), the adult percentage remains at 18%. The totals indicated above thus suggest a 'middle-class' adult population that was never less than 1,185 (i) or 890 (ii) and never more than 2,370 (i) or 1,780 (ii); of these, not less than 200 (i) or 150 (ii) and not more than 400 (i) or 300 (ii) will have been entitled in any given year to the possibly 'upper-middle-class' rite of cremation without grave goods. Both sexes are covered by these figures; open questions include the respective proportions at any stage between 750 and 700 of Euboeans by birth, Euboeans by descent, Euboeans by marriage (such as the 'native wives' once postulated by Buchner: ch. 4.4, s.v. *personal ornaments*) and resident aliens.

The consumption of any of these figures should be accompanied by a good many grains of salt, for they are inextricably bound up with several unwarranted assumptions: first, that the density of late eighth-century graves throughout the Pithekoussai cemetery is uniformly as high as it is in the sample covered by *Pithekoussai* I and reviewed in chapter 4; secondly, that the population remained stable throughout the period concerned; thirdly, that no category of the population was denied burial in the Valle di San Montano; and fourthly, that the burial of non-residents *was* denied there. It is hard to decide which of these propositions is the most unlikely. Nevertheless, the calculations expounded as briefly as possible in this section may at least serve to assist appreciation of the basic fact that Euboean Pithekoussai was never small. I do not understand how Morris (1987, 166 citing Ridgway 1984a, 64) derives a Pithekoussan population of '4,000 – 5,000 by 700 BC' from the first edition of this book, where I estimated that between 1,500 and 2,500 Pithekoussans were cremated between 750 and 700. The fact remains that an overall population that was always numbered in thousands rather than hundreds is not an unreasonable estimate for a settlement that even in its earliest stages has yielded abundant evidence of varied human activity over the far from negligible surface area summarily illustrated on Fig. 5.

However tantalizing the random selection of knowledge that archaeology has been able to retrieve since 1952 at Pithekoussai, there is no doubt that the variety, quality and quantity of the eighth-century evidence there have no contemporary parallels in the Greek and Etrusco-Italic worlds that Pithekoussai did so much to bring together. How this momentous and far reaching effect was achieved is the subject of the third and final part of this book.

*Part three*

# Interactions

# 6    Pithekoussai: status and function

... both lifeline and source of information

(Murray 1980, 100)

Before we can examine the interaction between the first Western Greeks and the native peoples of the Italian peninsula, we must make some attempt to define the significance of the first Western Greek base, Pithekoussai, in its own right. Accordingly, this chapter will address two fundamental questions. One concerns the status of Pithekoussai: was it a Euboean trading settlement (*emporion*) or a full-blown colony (*apoikia*)? The other question concerns Pithekoussai's function: to what extent may the Eretrians and Chalcidians who reached Ischia in the eighth century be credited with the forging of a definitive link between East and West? As we shall see in the two final chapters, both these questions are of immense significance for the later history of ancient Italy, and hence of Western civilization as a whole.

## 1    *Emporion* or *apoikia*?

Much discussion has revolved around the precise definitions of the terms 'trading settlement' and 'colony' (Mele 1979), and around the application of one or the other to Pithekoussai (Frederiksen 1979, 282–94). What then of the process that may now be assigned there, even more emphatically than before, to the first half of the eighth century on the basis of the minute quantity of imported Euboean and Corinthian Middle Geometric chevron skyphos sherds (Fig. 21; ch. 5.1) identified in the acropolis dump on Monte di Vico? Do they signal the beginning of trade or the raising of a flag? Should we conclude that the oldest graves in the cemetery of the first Western Greek establishment have still to be discovered? Or may we assume that they were all dismantled at a later stage, in the manner described in chapter 4.3? As we shall see in the next section of this chapter, if Pithekoussai was fully operational at the time of the chevron skyphoi, it would probably have blocked the trickle of contemporary Oenotrian Geometric into Southern Etruria. Since it clearly did not do so, I am tempted to define the Middle Geometric material from Monte di Vico as the outward and visible sign of a Euboean advance party, still in the process of establishing the Pithekoussan monopoly of Tyrrhenian trade that was characteristic of the second half of the eighth century.

Once the Pithekoussan community had been established, my own view is that both the 'trading settlement' (*emporion*) and the 'colony' (*apoikia*) definitions may be applied to it with varying degrees of accuracy. The nature, as distinct from the bulk, of the archaeological evidence so far retrieved at Pithekoussai is limited: nevertheless, it leads me to wonder just how important the *emporion/apoikia* distinction was to the actual denizens of eighth-century Pithekoussai – and whether indeed an original trading settlement there could not simply have evolved into a colony. If this suggestion seems unduly heretical (or naïve), I would plead that the dangers of rigid classification, notorious even among later Greek establishments overseas (Graham 1964, 4–8; Murray 1980, 104), are likely to be even greater in the case of the *first* such establishment (see Dunbabin 1948, 451 note 2 on 'frontier life'). After all, literacy and art of a high order were present at Pithekoussai from an early stage and on a scale that almost compels us to regard this centre as a 'special case'.

At this point, I should like to illustrate the difficulties that I have encountered in the search for a less anodyne word than 'establishment' to define the status of Pithekoussai in the second half of the eighth century. *Emporia* tend to be of mixed or uncertain parentage and to be characterized by mixed populations. Al Mina, Naucratis, Adria and Spina satisfy both these conditions; Pithekoussai satisfies only the second (and that to an arguably limited degree) by virtue of the Oriental residents who will be postulated later in this chapter. *Apoikie* on the other hand are self-sufficient (because food-producing) city-states abroad; as such, they are a product of the world of the Greek *polis* with all its attendant social implications. That there was a degree of social, indeed urban, organization at Pithekoussai from the middle of the eighth century onwards cannot be doubted: the sheer size of the settlement makes it inevitable. But it is hard to believe that the *polis* concept was already packaged for export at the first available opportunity, along with the Euboean and Corinthian Middle Geometric chevron skyphoi referred to in chapter 5.1; more than a generation later, in the 730s, Corinth herself was no more than a group of villages (Roebuck 1972). In any case, it is far from obvious that the social arrangements archaeologically perceptible at eighth-century Pithekoussai are exclusive to the *polis*, or to full-blown colonial status. Local dispositions concerning the siting (and doubtless the conduct) of the suburban Blacksmiths' Quarter or the delimitation and dismantling of family plots in the cemetery are practical matters, and surely no more socially significant than the physical choice of an easily defended site for the acropolis. Pioneers in a strange land – which is what the first generation of Euboeans at Pithekoussai were – are inevitably required to solve new problems on an *ad hoc* basis, and the resulting phenomena should not automatically be derived from pre-existing institutions in the country of origin. On the contrary, one of the most stimulating questions ever asked about Pithekoussai is precisely this: 'Is it possible that the example of the colonies [sic] may have accelerated developments at home?' (Snodgrass 1977, 33). If the answer to this question is in the affirmative, the undisputed status of Cumae and of most of the Sicilian foundations as *poleis* makes good sense, as does the subsequent transmission of the *polis* concept to the Etruscans. It remains true that M. Pallottino's classic description of the social group that wielded the main power in the Etruscan *poleis* is strikingly reminiscent of the situation at Pithekoussai two centuries earlier; he once referred to a 'class of sophisticated and hard-headed businessmen' at Volsinii (modern Orvieto), where ninety different families are attested epigraphically in the Crocefisso del Tufo cemetery between 550 and 500 (Pallottino 1951–3). As it happens, there is also onomastic evidence for a sixth-century Celtic penetration at Volsinii to match the earlier resident Orientals discussed below at Pithekoussai (De Simone 1978).

On the Bay of Naples, and perhaps in the West generally, the process of urbanization may reasonably be compared with that in contemporary Ionia. Although the reorganization of Smyrna after the presumed earthquake around 700 gave rise to the first certain and unambiguous apparition of the Greek *polis*, the first wall circuit there dates to the mid-ninth and the second to the mid-eighth century. Both represent public undertakings of considerable proportions, and the impression of an organized community is borne out by the densely packed structures of the eighth-century habitation: between four and five hundred families on a peninsula that was barely one-third (365 m) as long as the axis of Late Geometric I Pithekoussai (J. M. Cook et al. 1959).

## 2 Pithekoussai between East and West

From the 1950s onwards, the part played by the Euboeans in the early history of the Mediterranean has come to resemble that of a missing link between East and West. Accordingly, it seems appropriate to review the rise and fall – and partial re-emergence – of the Euboeans' predecessors in this important role: the Phoenicians. At one time, they were credited with an active presence over the vast area between Cornwall and Zimbabwe, and were further identified as the source of nearly everything that was good in the civilization of Greece. Then came the discoveries of Schliemann at

Troy and Mycenae, and with them the demonstrably autochthonous origins of classical Greece. As a result, hypotheses concerning the supposed Phoenician influence were summarily rejected: Salamon Reinach published *Le mirage oriental* in 1893; Julius Beloch, in the second edition of his *Griechische Geschichte* (1913), demolished the entire classical tradition of Phoenician greatness, and denied both the importance and – crucially – the chronological priority of their activities in the Western areas colonized by the Greeks (Albright 1941). Twenty years later, the history of Greek colonization began to acquire a new first chapter with the writings of Alan Blakeway (1933, 1935, 1936), who demonstrated the importance of Euboeo-Cycladic 'trade before the flag' – in the teeth of considerable opposition (Ridgway 1990a, 61); it was not long before evidence for a similarly early Greek presence, subsequently identified as Euboean, in the Near East was found by (Sir) Leonard Woolley at Al Mina (Ridgway 1973, 6–10); Giorgio Buchner's excavations at Euboean Pithekoussai on the Bay of Naples began in 1952 (Buchner 1954a), when (Sir) John Boardman (1952, 1957) was reviewing the then exiguous evidence for the Geometric period in Euboea itself (where the large-scale excavation of Lefkandi and Eretria began in the early 1960s).

Thus it was that modern discoveries in the Eastern and Western Mediterranean provided an acceptable Euboean substitute for the Phoenicians, long since deprived of their traditional role in the promotion of East–West relations. By 1977, however, it was possible for the late Martin Frederiksen to assert that 'the Phoenicians are on the way back' (Frederiksen 1977, 43). Something of what he meant was discussed in chapter 2.4, with particular reference to Sardinia. In the Italian peninsula, the excavations at Francavilla Marittima in Calabria have produced more evidence. There, for example, three noble Oenotrians of the first half of the eighth century were buried with numerous products of an unexpectedly advanced local metal industry that clearly derives its inspiration and techniques from the Phoenician world (Zancani Montuoro 1976). A decorated bronze bowl from a mid-eighth-century context at the same site (Zancani Montuoro 1971) has recently been authoritatively identified as 'a local copy or imitation of a Phoenician original' (Markoe 1985, 143; his Ca 1); the only incontrovertibly imported example so far known in Italy of the type imitated comes from Vetulonia in Tuscany (Maggiani 1973), and testifies further to 'the existence of Phoenician commercial ties with Etruria, Southern Italy, and Sicily during the middle and third quarter of the eighth century' (Markoe 1985, 145; his E 15). The geographical position of Francavilla is ideally suited both for exchanges with the outside world and for the exploitation of the internal routes, especially those that link the Ionian and Tyrrhenian seaboards. It is not surprising that Francavilla in Calabria and Vetulonia in

Tuscany are among the relatively few Italian sites outside Euboean Campania that have yielded seals of the North Syrian or Cilician Lyre-Player Group represented so abundantly at Pithekoussai (Vetulonia: Buchner and Boardman 1966, 26 no. 43bis; Francavilla: Boardman 1990b, 12 no. 44ter and the Notes to ch. 4.4).

Before the foundation of Pithekoussai, then, Sardinia and Calabria combine to demonstrate the independent presence of Levantine entrepreneurs in Italian waters. It is worth adding, too, that a few pieces of native Oenotrian Geometric pottery found their way from South Italy to Southern Etruria. As in the case of the Sardinian items in the same area, we shall never know who actually brought them: but the pattern of its distribution there has much in common with that of pre-colonial chevron skyphoi of Euboean type (ch. 7.2), and has accordingly been seen as indicating 'a degree of competition inconceivable *after* the foundation of Pithekoussai, given the monopoly exercised by this centre over Tyrrhenian trade' (Colonna 1974a, 298). It does not, however, follow that the Euboeans were either the first or the only merchant-venturers who were responsible for opening up the West.

## 3 Oriental residents at Pithekoussai

Like the multinational centre of Al Mina on the coast of North Syria, Euboean Pithekoussai on the Bay of Naples was of vital significance to any eighth-century group engaged in long-distance trade in the Mediterranean. That Pithekoussai really was established by Euboeans is not in doubt, nor yet is the demonstrable fact that Pithekoussai ushers in a momentous period of effective Hellenic interaction with the native peoples along the Tyrrhenian coast. Nevertheless, as we have seen (ch. 5.1), the physical situation of the first Western Greek acropolis is startlingly reminiscent of the 'promontories and small islands' (Thucydides 6.2) preferred by the Phoenicians for their foundations in Sicily and Sardinia. It almost looks as if the Euboeans had Phoenician advice in the selection of a suitable location. Whether they did or not, Pithekoussai has produced clear evidence not only for commercial contacts with the Levant but also – and from the earliest period so far attested in its history – for actual Levantine residents. The clearest proof of their presence is constituted by an imported amphora reused in an *enchytrismos* burial (grave 575) of the Late Geometric I period.

The amphora in question, 575–1, is of Greek type and bears three separate Semitic inscriptions (Fig. 29). Two of them, identified as Aramaic, define the original function of the amphora as a container of '200 [units of liquid]', being 'double [the standard quantity]'. F. Durando has calculated the physical capacity of the amphora, excluding the neck, at 54.826 litres;

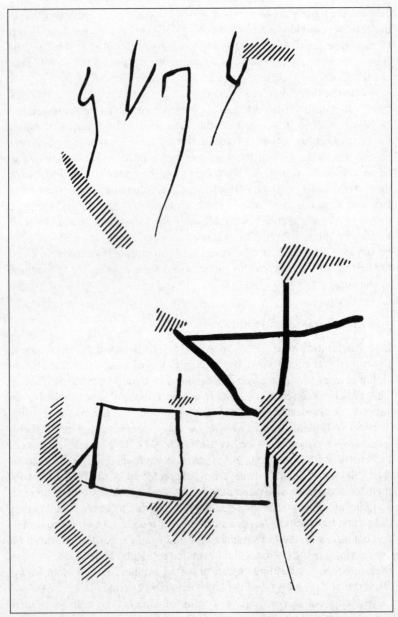

**Fig. 29.** Pithekoussai: the cemetery in the Valle di San Montano. Graffiti on amphora 575–1 (Late Geometric I; Buchner 1978, fig. 2). *Top*: Aramaic KPLN. *Bottom*: Semitic funerary symbol superimposed on Aramaic numeral indicating 200 (standard units).

the 200 standard units would thus be remarkably close to the Ionic-Attic kotyle (between 0·273 and 0·274 litre: Durando 1989, 81–4 with references). As recorded on amphora 575–1, this information has all the literary qualities of an ancient customs declaration – one that was presumably made at the point whence the amphora was despatched, and quite possibly by someone who had reason to expect that what he was writing would be understood at the intended Western destination. The language in which the information is conveyed indicates a linguistic area that was intimately connected with the development of written Aramaic while at the same time absorbing significant Phoenician influence. In other words, the author of these two inscriptions might well have learnt to write in precisely the same part of the Levant that sent, by one route or another, the numerous Lyre-Player Group seals encountered in other Late Geometric I graves at Pithekoussai (Figs. 15, 38). At first sight, indeed, it is tempting to suppose that the amphora was inscribed and despatched to Euboean Pithekoussai from Al Mina itself, where there were surely Euboean residents – and probably Euboean (or Euboean-trained) potters (Boardman 1959). They, however, would hardly have used Semitic writing to label their amphora. Accordingly, it is worth considering another possibility: that the amphora was despatched to the West not from Al Mina but from the island of Rhodes. One site, Ialysos, was held by later Rhodian historians to be the most important centre of Phoenician settlement (*FGrHist* iiib, 513, 523) on Rhodes; and J. N. Coldstream (1969, cf. 1972) has argued convincingly for a strong interest on the part of the Phoenician community in the international unguent trade from the mid-ninth century onwards. In the fullness of time, this accounts for the wide distribution, after about 725, of the *Kreis- und Wellenbandstil* aryballoi, of which there are well over 80 in the Late Geometric II graves catalogued in *Pithekoussai I*. The units employed to express the quantity of liquid conveyed in amphora 575–1 are small for wine, amounting in modern terms to no more than the normal individual serving (the Italian *quartino*). It is at least possible that an altogether more precious liquid was involved: it could be that the bulk transport of unguents from the Levant (Rhodes) was already taking place in the Pithekoussan Late Geometric I period, and that it was only in Late Geometric II that this valuable commodity was bottled and sealed at the source indicated by the distinctive Early Protocorinthian and *Kreis- und Wellenbandstil* aryballoi. Packaging is, after all, a well-known feature of commercial rivalry – and Corinthian competition is conspicuous by its absence in Late Geometric I.

It is thus not impossible that, shortly after the middle of the eighth century, the Phoenicians of Rhodes (where the Nestor kotyle was also made) had established some kind of contact with Pithekoussai that enabled them to despatch an amphora (or more probably a cargo of amphoras) containing some precious liquid to a compatriot there. Whatever the circumstances of the arrival of amphora 575–1, the nature of its third Semitic sign is clear enough: deliberately superimposed on the numeral, this roughly drawn triangle is identified as an 'all-purpose' Semitic religious symbol, well known in Phoenician and Punic contexts all over the Mediterranean (Falsone 1978), and obviously related to the secondary – funerary – function of amphora 575–1 as the container of the pathetic remains of a dead baby. Around 740, this amphora, bearing this symbol, was deposed in a family plot at Euboean Pithekoussai. The conclusion is inescapable: at least one of the occupant's parents felt bound to observe non-Greek, Levantine usage – and was therefore most probably of non-Greek, Levantine origin. The ecumenical aspect of this event is perhaps unexpected, and begs a great many questions: they may conveniently be added to those raised by the more or less contemporary urn, probably made at Pithekoussai, certainly painted in the Euboean Late Geometric manner – and used in the Phoenician rites observed in the *tophet* at Sulcis in Sardinia (see the Notes on further reading to ch. 5.3).

The family plot that included *enchytrismos* grave 575 consisted of a cremation burial under a tumulus (grave 199) of the Late Geometric I period; this partly covered a trench grave (574), the preparation of which had destroyed the lower part of the inscribed amphora used for the *enchytrismos* 575. Tumulus 199 was also found to overlay a second trench grave (577) without grave goods and a second *enchytrismos* burial (grave 578; also without goods), this time in an amphora of the common local type. Amphora 575–1 itself contained a small bronze ring, a bone pendant in the form of a double axe and a scarab. Trench grave 574 belonged to a small boy aged approximately eight and a half; he had been interred with two fine seals of the Lyre-Player Group (Buchner and Boardman 1966, 5 no. 4; 7 no. 7), and a local oinochoe of Late Geometric I type. The cremation under tumulus 199 was that of a female adult, with a pair of gold-plated silver hair rings, a silver ribbed bracelet and another local Late Geometric I oinochoe. The family is thus represented by a mother, two babies, a young son and perhaps – in the trench grave without goods – a servant or retainer. The father's grave has not survived: it is reasonable to suppose that a tumulus covering the cremation of a male adult was originally sited next to tumulus 199. The plot is unfortunately situated in a particularly deep part of the Valle San Montano cemetery, and there are traces of later clearance and reuse in the form of two modest cremations of the seventh century; sadly, their presence has probably deprived us of a cremation burial that we would have been able to identify as almost certainly that of an adult male of Levantine origin.

The presence of other early Levantine residents may be inferred from

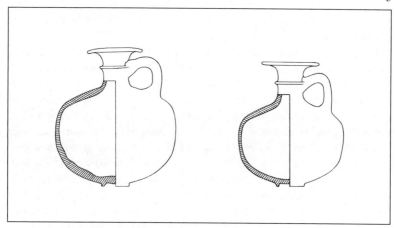

**Fig. 30.** Pithekoussai: the cemetery in the Valle di San Montano. Levantine aryballoi 166–5, –8 (Late Geometric I; Buchner 1982b, fig. 2; associated with the Argive Monochrome lekythos, Pl. 5, *top centre*).

three categories of artefact, clearly imported from the East, that occur in the Pithekoussan graves of the Late Geometric I period: Lyre-Player Group seals (Figs. 15, 38); scarabs; and the so-called 'Levantine' aryballoi (Fig. 30), probably imported from Rhodes (like the *Kreis- und Wellenbandstil* aryballoi of the Pithekoussan Late Geometric II period). Of the sample examined in chapter 4, the total number of Late Geometric I graves containing at least one of these items is thirty – just over a third of the 750–725 cemetery population whose mortal remains and grave goods are published in *Pithekoussai I*. It would be rash in the extreme to conclude that *all* these individuals were themselves Levantines: but the proportion of graves containing at least one Levantine import is high, and speaks volumes for the extent to which early Pithekoussai was permeated by Levantine contacts and influences.

The example of one family plot must suffice. In funerary terms, the family in question was founded by a cremation tumulus with characteristically male grave goods (167); next to it was a similar burial (166) with female goods – presumably the wife of the first. Both sets of grave goods are distinguished by the conspicuous quantity of precious metal, Levantine aryballoi (Fig. 30) and – in the case of the woman – by the presence of impasto pottery, which is extremely rare in cremations. Giorgio Buchner's description of grave 166 in *Pithekoussai I* includes the following suggestion: 'the rich personal ornaments that denote membership of an upper class contrast sharply with the modest oinochoe, worn and chipped by long service. Perhaps it is not too fanciful to suppose that in this case it was a devoted slave who used his own humble jug to pour the last libation on the pyre of his mistress.'

Under the cremation burials 166 and 167, a number of inhumations in trench graves contain silver items – which are 'abnormal' in children's graves like these, as we saw in chapter 4.5. It seems at least possible that this unusual group of Late Geometric I depositions represents the family of a non-Greek (and most probably Levantine) couple, who, in a period when Greek aryballoi were unknown, used Levantine ones – the oldest examples of the form in the whole of Magna Graecia. This group is the most conspicuous of the Pithekoussan family plots with Late Geometric I graves containing one or more Levantine items. In the Late Geometric II period, a member of the same family cremated his ten-year-old son (instead of inhuming him, as we should expect) and buried him in grave 168 with two impasto vases (as noted above, these are rare in cremations) and the finest collection of local and imported painted pottery yet found in any grave in the Valle San Montano cemetery: Early Protocorinthian and *Kreis- und Wellenbandstil* aryballoi, no less than four kraters – and the Nestor kotyle (Figs. 7, 8).

At first sight, it may seem heretical to suggest that the Greek verses inscribed on the Nestor kotyle (Fig. 9) belonged to a family that was partly of non-Greek, Levantine extraction. In fact, it makes perfectly good sense in the context of Pithekoussai and of the contemporary Mediterranean. There is, after all, no reason to believe that the verses were composed and inscribed by a member of the family involved: the author of this decidedly non-funereal ditty (see the Notes on further reading to ch. 4.4) was clearly a Euboean, like most of the inhabitants of Pithekoussai in the second half of the eighth century. It could just be, too, that the incidence of *orientalia* and precious metal (silver) in the first generation of the family indicates simply that then, as later, its members were exceptionally well-to-do Euboeans. On the other hand, the alternative explanation – a Levantine component in the family's origin – is surely even more likely, not least in view of the solemn ritual (and hence probably ethnic) implications of the Levantine aryballoi and of the no less significant commercial implications of their contents. In the *Pithekoussai I* assemblage, there are twenty-one Late Geometric I adult cremations with grave goods, three of which yielded Levantine aryballoi (Notes on further reading to ch. 4.4): this might well indicate the size (about 15%) of the Levantine group that was present in, and being absorbed by, the early Euboean population of Pithekoussai.

In the next generation, which is also that of the Nestor kotyle, a minute fragment (3 × 2·2 cm; Fig. 31, upper) of a locally made vase suggests the presence of another immigrant from the East. This sherd had strayed into the lens of black earth (brought from the funeral pyre in the circumstances

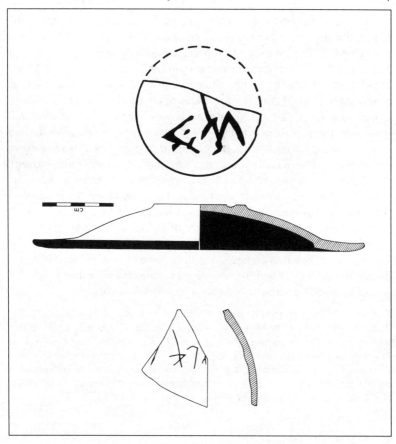

**Fig. 31.** Pithekoussai: Phoenician inscriptions (Buchner 1978, figs. 5, 6, 7). *Top*: on a stray sherd of a local kantharos of Early Protocorinthian type (as Pl. 6, *bottom right*), found in the lens of cremation 232 (Late Geometric II) in the Valle di San Montano cemetery. *Bottom*: on a Phoenician Red Slip plate from the acropolis dump, Monte di Vico.

explained in chapter 4.2) of the cremation tomb 232, which belongs to a comparatively late stage of the Late Geometric II period and can thus be dated to the last decade of the eighth century. The sporadic items in its lens of black earth need not be very much earlier; the vase to which the inscribed sherd belongs was almost certainly a locally imitated Early Protocorinthian kantharos of a type (as Pl. 6, bottom right) that is common in Late Geometric II graves. Only two complete letters survive of the inscription itself, which was once defined as 'perhaps the oldest inscription so far known in the Greek alphabet' (Guarducci 1964) following the identification of one of the letters as a 'sideways alpha' of an early type – too early, in fact, for the date that emerged from closer investigation of its context and typology. The subsequent proposal, advanced independently by two different scholars, one Italian (Rocco 1970) and one American (McCarter 1975), that this text be rotated through 180° and read as Phoenician, is confirmed beyond all doubt by the *ductus* of the letters: and since the sherd is part of a local vase, they must have been inscribed at Pithekoussai. Ironically, the American scholar's suspicions of the Greek identification were aroused by a mistaken reference to the fabric of this sherd as *rosso* (red: typically Phoenician): it is in fact *rosa* (pink: typically Pithekoussan). As it happens, another Phoenician inscription does occur on a character- istically red Phoenician plate from the acropolis dump on Monte di Vico (Fig. 31); it obviously cannot be dated by its context, but it is in all probability more or less contemporary with the sherd from grave 232.

The main evidence for speakers of the Semitic language known as Phoenician at Euboean Pithekoussai thus comes from the almost casual discovery of scraps of their writing. However unimpressive the evidence, it is hard to gainsay a shrewd observation by Giorgio Buchner:

It seems unlikely that [these examples] represent isolated cases. We should rather think in terms of the stable presence, throughout the second half of the eighth century, of a certain number of Levantines. If this was so, their residence at Pithekoussai must have been advantageous not only to themselves but also (and especially) to their Greek hosts. The most convincing explanation would appear to be that they were not merchants but craftsmen and artists, commissioned by the Greeks to work in the Orientalizing style. (Buchner 1978, 142)

## 4    Aftermath

Then ... comes Cumae, founded at a very early date by folk from Chalcis and [Euboean] Kyme; it is certainly the most ancient of all the Siceliot and Italiot foundations. The actual founders, Hippocles of Kyme and Megasthenes of Chalcis, agreed between themselves that Cumae should be a colony [*apoikia*] of Chalcis but take its name from Kyme: this is why the city is called Cumae, and generally regarded as a solely Chalcidian foundation. To begin with, the city was prosperous ... many traces still survive there of Greek manners and customs. (Strabo 5. 4. 4; see chapter 3.1 for the etymology of Cumae, and for the absence of any reference in this passage to Pithekoussai)

The earliest colonial finds at Cumae are Early Protocorinthian globular aryballoi and deep kotylai, contemporary with those encountered in the Late Geometric II graves in the Valle San Montano cemetery at Pithe- koussai and thus not earlier than the conventional date of 725. This will have to serve, now and for the forseeable future, as the date for the founda- tion of a new Greek *polis* on the mainland of Campania. It had none of the

natural disadvantages of Pithekoussai (isolation, earthquakes and eruptions: Strabo 5.4.9; ch. 3.1), and was therefore capable, in a way that
Pithekoussai was not, both of commercial expansion and of a degree of
agricultural exploitation of the surrounding territory (*chora*) comparable
with that operated at the first foundations far to the south in Sicily (for
example at Euboean Naxos from 734 and at Corinthian Syracuse from
733). There is as yet no evidence to support an attractive alternative
hypothesis, according to which 'the earliest colonial horizon has yet to be
recovered' at Cumae, implying a date for its foundation that 'must fall
somewhere within the bracket 760–735' (Coldstream 1977, 230). On present evidence, Pithekoussai in its Late Geometric I period (*c.* 750–725)
appears to be the only permanent Greek establishment in the West, and
hence a natural magnet for other foreigners, especially those who had
already been active in Western waters for some time.

Of these, the Euboeans of Pithekoussai would no doubt have used the
Greek word *Phoinikes* to describe the Levantine residents postulated in the
previous section. Writing of the non-conformist originality that distin-
guishes the well-known series of Sardinian bronze figurines, N. K. Sandars
once compared some of them to 'the perennial under-privileged frequenter
of quays whom you may meet today in any large Mediterranean port. It
almost looks as though a Sardinian artist were poking fun at the ubiquitous
Levantine trader . . .' (Sandars 1968, 220). It is hardly a coincidence that, as
A. Mele has pointed out, in the Homeric poems the Phoenicians are frequently encountered in ports; not all of them were under-privileged, for
they had 'the same customs of gift exchange and hospitality as the Greeks
[and] an explicit and important role in the production of artefacts in precious metal' (Mele 1979, 87). We may suppose that the Phoenicians were
soon joined, in the West as elsewhere, by refugees from the momentous
clashes in North Syria, the effects of which included the fall of Hama
around 720. It would not be surprising if, in the second half of the eighth
century, more than one Easterner thought of Euboean Pithekoussai in much
the same way as Demaratus of Corinth is said to have thought of Etruscan
Tarquinia in the second half of the seventh (Coldstream 1977, 242f.; and
see ch. 8); and we should not forget that the Hellenization of Etruria (with
which Demaratus had traded prior to his emigration there in 657: Dionysius
of Halicarnassus 3.46.3–5) owed a good deal to Cumae, the mainland
successor and heir to Pithekoussai. In this connection, another illuminating
observation by Mele deserves more attention than it has hitherto received:
that much of the traditional importance later ascribed to Cumae by ancient
writers of history in fact belongs to Pithekoussai (Mele 1979, 32).

In sum, many of the seeds of the orientalizing phenomenon that charac-
terizes the arts and crafts of mainland Campania, Latium vetus and Etruria

in the seventh century were sown at Pithekoussai prior to the end of the eighth. Meanwhile, of the effects on the Euboeans themselves of their long acquaintance with their Eastern neighbours, both in the East and in the West, one of the most striking is surely the adoption by the Euboean Cesnola Painter (Coldstream 1971) – alone among the Greek Geometric masters – of a key decorative motif that is of wholly Eastern derivation. Rampant goats flank the sacred tree on his masterpiece, the Cesnola krater in New York; the same motif occurs not only at Pithekoussai (on a local lekythos from a Late Geometric I grave: Fig. 11) but also on a 'barrel vase', now too in New York (Metropolitan inv. 1975.363; Ridgway 1977, 221), that was presumably made and found at Bisenzio, deep in the hinterland of Etruria.

Campania, Latium vetus and Southern Etruria
in the ninth and eighth centuries

---

> [T]he very great majority of the themes, types and motifs of Etruria's
> artistic production find their antecedents and inspiration in Greek
> models ... But there are differences: Etruria ignored certain Greek
> motifs, while developing others which met with little popularity in
> Greece or which belonged to styles that had already been discarded.
> There are also indications of attitudes foreign or even opposed to the
> figurative conceptions of the Greek world.
>
> (Pallottino 1978, 166)

In Part One of this book we established the identity of the first Western
Greeks (ch. 2) and of the island in the Bay of Naples to which they came
(ch. 3); in Part Two we reviewed at some length the evidence for what they
did when they got there. Part Three began with an assessment of our
findings (ch. 6). There should now be no doubt that the earliest Euboeans
so far found at Pithekoussai arrived with a formidable and fully formed
combination of taste, technology and Levantine connections: thanks to the
latter, there is a good case for regarding Pithekoussai as some kind of
'missing link' on the route from East to West, and the fact that this route
was demonstrably in use by the first half of the eighth century has considerable implications. The age-old question of Etruscan origins is among the
more important issues at stake: the connection between Etruria and the East
was effected not by the émigré 'Tyrrhene artificers' once envisaged by
D. Randall-MacIver (1927, ch. 7), but by the international community of
merchants and craftsmen resident at Pithekoussai; and Randall-MacIver's
'crucible ... situated somewhere in the Levant', so vital to the development
of art and culture in Etruria, was no further away than the Bay of Naples.
Our task in these two final chapters is thus to assess the impact that the
arrival and activities of the first Western Greeks made on the native peoples
of the Italian peninsula. For what cultural changes were the Euboeans
responsible, and what did they mean in human terms? We begin by resum-
ing the story that was broken off at the end of chapter 1: an examination of
Campania, Latium vetus and Southern Etruria in the ninth and eighth

centuries will prepare us for the consequences on the indigenous mainland of Pithekoussai's decline at the beginning of the seventh (ch. 8).

## 1  The native context

*Campania (Fig. 32)*

The effective discovery and excavation of Pithekoussai from the early 1950s were joined in the following decade by a no less remarkable and continuing boom in Iron Age discovery, excavation and exegesis on the mainland of Campania. The increase in our knowledge of this vital region at the stage that interests us here will be apparent to anyone who compares the Campanian section in H. Müller-Karpe's classic treatment of Urnfield chronology north and south of the Alps (Müller-Karpe 1959) with its counterpart in the brilliant synthesis of the Iron Age in Southern Italy and Sicily published only fifteen years later by B. d'Agostino (1974). For Müller-Karpe, there was only Cumae – in the form of graves and their contents that had been published over forty years previously (Gabrici 1913). D'Agostino was able to add a southerly extension of the initially cremating 'Villanovan' phenomenon, represented in Campania by the Capua and Pontecagnano groups and the Vallo di Diano 'aspect', to the inhuming culture represented by the Cumae and Oliveto-Cairano groups. The disentangling of the interactions between these five cultural entities – and between any and all of them and the outside world – continues to be hampered both by their lack of internal homogeneity and by the almost exclusively funerary nature of the evidence available for the period between the early ninth and the late eighth centuries.

Of the southern 'Villanovan' sites, the most northerly is Capua (Santa Maria Capua Vetere), destined for greatness as the chief city of Etruscan Campania. As Rome controlled the crossing of the Tiber, so Capua controlled that of the Volturnus at a natural crossroads: in particular, its situation at the southern end of the natural route that leads (via the Liri, Sacco and Tiber valleys) to Bisenzio explains the fact that Capua's principal Iron Age affinities are with Chiusi and the hinterland of Vulci in Southern Etruria. By the end of the eighth century, Pontecagnano (d'Agostino and Gastaldi 1988) was a great native emporium. The sites that make up its group (Pontecagnano itself, Arenosola and Capodifiume) are all within easy reach of the Gulf of Salerno; and evidence for early contact between them and the centres of south-east Sicily (Pantalica) and maritime Etruria (Caere, Tarquinia) comes as no surprise. On the showing of Sala Consilina (de La Genière 1968), the Vallo di Diano participated initially in the cultural manifestations of the two areas it separates, namely the Salernitano (the

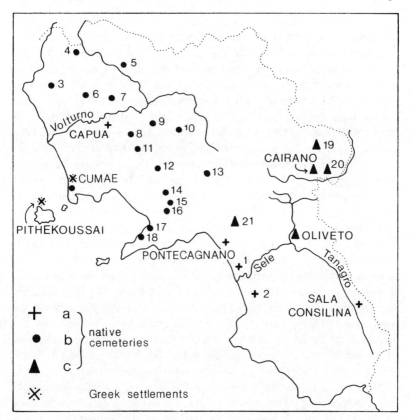

**Fig. 32.** Protohistoric cemeteries in Campania (after Gastaldi 1979, fig. 1).
**a:** *Villanovan* (in addition to Capua, Pontecagnano and Sala Consilina):
   **1:** Arenosola. **2:** Capodifiume.
**b:** *the inhuming Cumae group* (in addition to Cumae):
   **3:** Suessa. **4:** Presenzano. **5:** Allifae. **6:** Cales. **7:** Trebula. **8:** Calatia.
   **9:** Saticula. **10:** Caudium. **11:** Suessula. **12:** Nola. **13:** Avella. **14:** Striano.
   **15:** S. Valentino Torio. **16:** S. Marzano. **17:** Stabiae. **18:** Vico Equense.
**c:** *the inhuming Oliveto–Cairano group* (in addition to Oliveto and Cairano):
   **19:** Bisaccia. **20:** Calitri. **21:** Montecorvino Rovella.

Pontecagnano group) and Lucania (the modern administrative region of
Basilicata) – of which the latter, archaeologically speaking, was virtually
*terra incognita* (Dunbabin 1948, 153) until the creation of an autonomous
Archaeological Superintendency at Potenza in 1964. In the course of the
eighth century, this equilibrium gave way to a decided preference for the
interior, as a result of which Sala Consilina must henceforth be seen as an
integral part of Northern Lucania.

It is thus clear enough that the development of the 'Villanovan' centres of Campania was far from uniform; nevertheless, development there was. In sharp contrast, the cultural state of many centres aligned in the two groups – Cumae and Oliveto-Cairano – of the inhuming culture remained relatively static in the period that concerns us here, and indeed for long afterwards. This is particularly true of the Oliveto-Cairano group, of ultimately trans-Adriatic extraction: its characteristic hill-sites are found in the upper valleys of the Ofanto (Bisaccia, Calitri, Cairano) and the Sele (Oliveto Citra) and as far west as the Monti Picentini (Montecorvino Rovella), whence further progress towards the Tyrrhenian seaboard was presumably blocked by the presence in the Ager Picentinus of the 'Villanovan' Pontecagnano group. Detailed study of the eponymous centre of Cairano (Bailo Modesti 1980) reveals a destiny that could hardly differ more radically from that of Capua: as late as the sixth/fifth centuries, the Cairano settlement still cannot be defined as urban, and its tombs bear mute witness to the persistence of certain ceramic and bronze types for up to two centuries after their demise elsewhere. The survival of social structures of this frankly rustic type in both of the groups characterized by trench graves is clearly a result of their location, remote and difficult of access, in the depths of the rural interior. Of the sites that have been assigned to the Cumae group, and of which the material is also available for study in published form, Cumae itself and two cemeteries in the Valle del Sarno, S. Marzano and S. Valentino Torio (Gastaldi 1979), are not subject to these limitations.

Cumae is clearly a special case. Its *rocca*, which is normally within sight of the acropolis of Pithekoussai, surveys and controls access from the north to the Bay of Naples; and in turn it too became the acropolis of a Greek colony when the Euboeans established themselves on the mainland (Livy 8.22.5–6; ch. 3.1). The nature of the evidence regarding pre-Hellenic Cumae is highly unsatisfactory both in quality and quantity. It consists of no more than 36 graves excavated on the Orilia estate at the expense of E. Osta in the last century; their contents were eventually purchased by the Naples Museum, and eventually published by Gabrici in 1913. Müller-Karpe distinguished two phases in this exiguous assemblage and argued for a commencement of the sequence in the ninth century: a reasonable time had to be allowed for typological development from the first to the second phase, which was still earlier than the foundation of the Greek colony. Of more lasting value than the supposition of change in the cultural repertoire is the recognition of typological affinities between the impasto pottery of pre-Hellenic Cumae and that of Rome and Latium vetus in the century between approximately 850 and 750.

The limited evidence from Cumae has been supplemented by the excavations at S. Marzano (1968 onwards) and S. Valentino Torio (1974 onwards) in the Valle del Sarno. The trench graves at S. Marzano have yielded material in a range that begins in the ninth century; on present evidence, those of S. Valentino may be assigned to the period from the early eighth, and in the fullness of time both sites received painted pottery of Greek Late Geometric type, some of which was probably made at Pithekoussai (d'Agostino 1979). The excavations in the Valle del Sarno fall into the British 'urban rescue' category, effected in a densely populated area bounded by two motorways, and the settlements associated with these two interesting cemeteries continue to elude discovery. In spite of the valley's obvious economic importance (the Sarno is 'a river that transports cargoes both inland and down to the sea': Strabo 5.4.8), the status of S. Marzano and S. Valentino Torio does not seem to exceed that of the scattered village, abruptly arrested – for reasons that are far from clear – in the middle of the sixth century. Throughout, the trench grave surrounded by a horseshoe-shaped gully is characteristic of both cemeteries; this distinctive feature, unique in Campania, has been compared to Picene practice.

## Latium vetus (Fig. 33)

The cultural development of Campania in the ninth and eighth centuries is expressed above in terms of two distinct cultures, overlapping in space (notably in the Salernitano) as in time: that of cremating 'Villanovan' type, and that associated with inhumation in trench graves. The same elements are present in contemporary Latium vetus, north of the Garigliano and south of the Tiber. Here the keynote is not so much 'interaction' on Campanian lines as 'integration' in the period that followed the relative isolation that had characterized the local cultural record down to the middle of the ninth century. The next hundred years or so – the 'second Latial period' of the conventional chronological sequence – are a complex but vital period in the history of Latium. In it, two phases have been distinguished, of which some have seen in the first (IIA: mid- to late ninth century) a predominance of 'Villanovan' affinities, while in the second (IIB: late ninth to mid-eighth) the southern influence of the Campanian inhuming culture appears to be in the ascendant. The equation of cultural features, archaeologically perceived, with the ethnic identities sought by the historian is inherently dangerous. Nevertheless, it is tempting to see an indigenous Latin population behind those aspects of material culture that are akin to the Villanovan of contemporary Southern Etruria; the subsequent admission of features that recall contemporary Campania then suggests an intrusion that can be matched with the Sabine component in the traditional version of the dual origin of Rome itself.

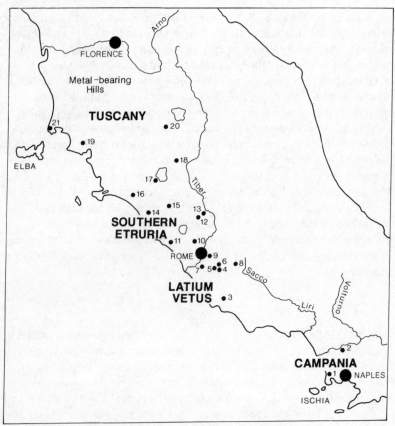

**Fig. 33.** Protohistoric Campania, Latium vetus and Etruria: main sites.
**1:** Cumae. **2:** Capua. **3:** Satricum. **4:** Marino. **5:** Castelgandolfo. **6:** Grottaferrata.
**7:** Castel di Decima. **8:** Palestrina (Praeneste). **9:** La Rustica. **10:** Veii. **11:** Caere.
**12:** Narce. **13:** Falerii Veteres. **14:** Tarquinia. **15:** Vetralla. **16:** Vulci. **17:** Bisenzio.
**18:** Orvieto (Volsinii Veteres). **19:** Vetulonia. **20:** Chiusi. **21:** Populonia.

However this may be, the *caesura* that has been detected in the topographical development of the Rome cemeteries around the end of the ninth century is clearly a crucial one: in the conventional sequence, it separates IIA (which is a continuation of I) from IIB (which continues in III), and is accompanied by important realignments elsewhere in Latium. The sum total of the processes involved amounts to a substantial change in the manner of inhabiting territory: it resembles, but is slower than, the revolution that is taking place in the mainstream and coastal centres of contemporary Southern Etruria. At the beginning of the ninth century, the network of independent and conspicuously non-urban hill-villages centred on ancient

Alba Longa (modern Castelgandolfo) and extending as far as Marino and Grottaferrata represents the Latium of the *triginta populi Albenses* – of which Pliny's list (*NH* 3.69) does not include Rome. During the eighth century, the decline of the Alban Hills system coincides with the growth of Rome to fill an urban area that to all intents and purposes heralds that of the period of the Etruscan kings (traditionally 616–509). In other words, Rome takes the lead in Latium; by the end of the period under review it is self-evidently a notable centre of population, and as such comparable with its distinguished contemporaries to the south (Capua), to the north (Veii, Caere, Tarquinia) and further north still (Bologna).

## Southern Etruria (Fig. 33)

We turn now to the source of those cultural aspects referred to as 'Villano-van' in the above brief outlines of indigenous developments in Campania and Latium vetus in the ninth and eighth centuries. There were no such people as 'the Villanovans'; any degree of indigenous ethnic unity that underlies the Villanovan *culture* must be attributed to the Etruscans them-selves in the Iron Age phase of their development. The point, though simple, is of fundamental importance to our purpose here; it is assumed in this and in the following chapter that the Etruscans took on their historical aspect by a process of 'ethnic formation' (Pallottino 1978, 78) between the Tiber and the Arno, and that the final stages of this gradual transformation can be detected in the archaeological record of the Villanovan culture there during the ninth and the eighth centuries. The external appearance of the Villanovan phenomenon varies considerably between the areas where it is represented, and indeed from site to site within each area. As we saw in chapter 1.2, this degree of cultural variation strongly suggests the exist-ence, already in the Iron Age, of a cantonal condition not unlike that of the historical Etruscan civilization itself. Consideration of Southern Etruria at this time may conveniently be divided between the coastal or mainstream centres on the one hand and the interior on the other. Not surprisingly, the pace of change is faster in the former than it is in the latter.

The emergence of the Villanovan culture on the mainstream sites of Southern Etruria is typified by the case of Veii, where 651 graves were excavated by Rome University and the British School at Rome in the Quattro Fontanili cemetery between 1961 and 1972 and published in cata-logue form between 1963 and 1976. The uniquely accessible mass of data thus afforded for the structure of Veientine society is not easy to interpret in detail; but it seems reasonable in the first instance to infer the existence of distinct communities from the presence of other, separate cemeteries exca-vated in the early years of the present century and still, alas, substantially unpublished (1,200 tombs were dug at Veii between 1913 and 1916 alone). Each cemetery at Veii is sited on raised ground around the central area, and each yielded its earliest tombs at the highest point (Ward Perkins 1961, pl. 32); the extent to which the hypothetical Veientine communities reflected by these cemeteries were linked is clearly still a matter for the further research that must follow the long-awaited publication of more evidence. For the moment, we are probably justified in describing Veii, along with the other major centres that were growing on previously uninhabited sites elsewhere in Southern Etruria, as 'proto-urban' in view both of their sheer size and of their demonstrable demographic superiority over the sites of the Final Bronze Age. The advent of the Villanovan in Southern Etruria signals nothing less than a revolution in the manner of inhabiting territory; as we have seen, its effect was felt in Latium too.

The growth of densely populated centres in the ninth century had certain predictable repercussions in the eighth. The material of this date from the Quattro Fontanili cemetery at Veii and from the contemporary cemeteries at Tarquinia supports a hypothesis of greater stability in settlement; it is accompanied by a significant degree of specialization (or even industrialization) in ceramic and metallurgical production techniques, and by greater scope for short- and long-range commercial exchange mechanisms. Towards the end of the eighth century (*c.* 720), we are approaching a stage in which the funerary evidence is sophisticated enough to express social differentiation in death. This is a tenable deduction from the presence in the graves of the Quattro Fontanili and other cemeteries at Veii and elsewhere in Southern Etruria of the equipment necessary for the exercise of the martial arts (helmets, shields and swords; Figs. 35 and 36), the personal adornment of females (fibulas and other personal ornaments), feasting (after cooking and roasting on fire-dogs) and the ritual preparation and consumption of the beverages prescribed for special occasions (fine pottery). The graves that are endowed with unusually rich selections of these sophisticated products of advanced manufacturing techniques (see also Fig. 37) may surely be assigned to a nascent social élite, an élite that will in time find funerary expression in the form and contents of the orientalizing 'princely' graves in Etruria no less than in Latium vetus (whence Pl. 14) and Campania.

The principal difference between the early Villanovan stage in the hinterland and at the mainstream centres like Tarquinia and Veii appears to reside in a different relationship with what has gone before: continuity and gradual change in the interior, *caesura* and radical reorganization on the coast. Thus Bisenzio, well inland, is characterized in the ninth century by a multiplicity of scattered settlements, not yet centralized, that suggests a much slower transition from the Final Bronze to the Early Iron Age than anything that happened near the coast. In sharp contrast, relations between Bisenzio and Vulci acquire particular significance during the eighth century; and at Bisenzio itself the funerary material displays a wide range of flourishing external contacts. We have already seen that these include Capua, far to the south in Campania but accessible via the natural north-south land route along the Tiber, Sacco and Liri valleys. The result of this relationship with the outside world is seen to good effect in the considerable qualitative differences between the eighth-century repertoires encountered at Bisenzio and at the sites that face it across Lake Bolsena; it has even been suggested that the differences in question herald the much later territorial distinction between the Roman *municipia* of Visentium and Volsinii (Colonna 1973, 63). Meanwhile, however, at Bisenzio and in the Etruscan hinterland generally, the promise of a brilliant future is not fulfilled; and the seventh century sees a reversion to the slower pace characteristic of the ninth, expressed not least in the dull and frankly uninspired production of ceramic lines outmoded elsewhere.

## 2 The first contacts with the Euboeans

The previous section reviewed, however summarily, the rich and varied cultural panorama that was unfolding along the west (or Tyrrhenian) coast of central Italy during the ninth and eighth centuries. For all the differences in origin and development between the three regions considered, certain notable advances were registered in at least some parts of all of them during this vital period: the achievement of centralized proto-urban settlement; the emergence of embryonic social differentiation; the development of craft specialization to a degree that may be defined as industrial. It would be unduly simplistic to attribute progress of this order entirely to the arrival of the Euboeans in the area, and to their establishment of a base on Ischia. No less simplistic would be the assumption that the activities of literate, technologically advanced and commercially inclined foreigners had no effect whatsoever on the progress of the native peoples with whom they undoubtedly came into contact. Before attempting to decide at what point between these two extremes the nearest approximation to the truth may lie, it will be as well to describe the evidence for initial contact – of whatever sort – between Greeks and natives in Campania, Latium vetus and Etruria prior to the end of the eighth century.

In Campania, three skyphoi of Euboean type with painted chevrons disposed horizontally in the handle zone have long been known. They were found in two of the 36 pre-Hellenic graves at Cumae (Osta 3 and 29: Close-Brooks and Ridgway 1979, 113 fig. 6a-c), and clearly belong to the same chronological horizon (Euboean Middle Geometric) as the minute quantity

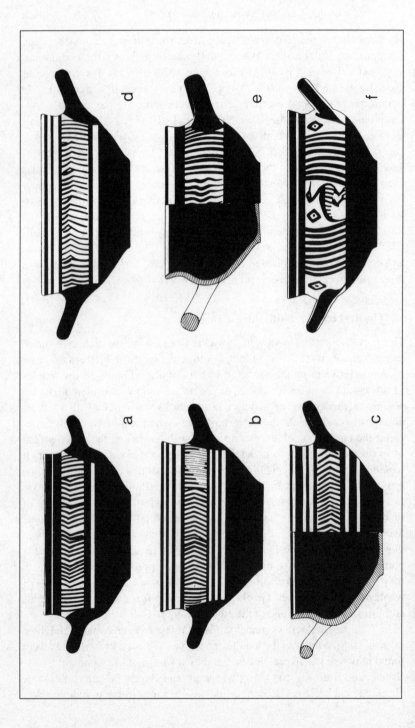

of sherds of similar skyphoi found in the acropolis dump at Pithekoussai (ch. 5.1; Fig. 21); so too do the chevron skyphoi from Capua, Pontecagnano, other sites in Campania and above all the Quattro Fontanili and Grotta Gramiccia Villanovan cemeteries at Veii in Southern Etruria (Close-Brooks and Ridgway 1979, 113–23). At the latter centre, careful stylistic analysis of the chevron skyphoi (Descoeudres and Kearsley 1983) has led to a conclusion that is not unlike that proposed by the present writer (Ridgway 1981a) for their counterparts at Pithekoussai: most of them are imported from Euboea, specifically from Eretria, and there is one from Corinth in the Grotta Gramiccia cemetery (Fig. 34a; Bartoloni 1990). Descoeudres further concluded that it was no longer possible to suppose (with Close-Brooks and Ridgway 1979, 119) that skyphoi imported from Greece preceded locally made versions in the native Veientine sequence. If, however, the Quattro Fontanili pieces examined by Descoeudres are arranged according to the order in which their graves occur in the convincing seriation of the native material subsequently achieved by J. Toms (1986), a reasonable measure of confirmation emerges for the imported-local succession – so long as Descoeudres' stylistic identifications are maintained: the 'Style' column on Table 6 (which is adapted from Ridgway 1988a, 498–502) shows that the principal exception is the Veientine chevron skyphos (Fig. 34c) associated with a supposedly Cycladic example of the same type (Fig. 34b) in grave FF 16–17. On the other hand, many of Descoeudres' stylistic diagnoses have since been called into question by Mössbauer (i.e. physical) analysis of the clay of a number of Quattro Fontanili pieces (Deriu et al. 1985): ten that had been examined in detail by Descoeudres and three more (identified in Table 6 by an asterisk*) that he attributed to 'a potter who came to Veii from Greece (and most probably from Euboea) and who adapted, in course of time, some native features' (Descoeudres and Kearsley 1983, 30f. note 68). If these alternative identities are also arranged in the order indicated by Toms' diagnosis of the native associations of the pieces concerned, as they are in Table 6, it will readily be seen that the imported-local succession is not supported by clay analysis.

The more or less contemporary occurrence in the Quattro Fontanili graves at Veii of chevron skyphoi identified (by clay analysis) as Eretrian, Western and Veientine is entirely consonant with the presence in the eighth century not only of imported Euboean pottery but also of at least one

**Fig. 34.** Geometric skyphoi from the Villanovan cemeteries at Veii (Close–Brooks and Ridgway 1979, figs. 6 and 7). **a:** Grotta Gramiccia, grave 779. **b–f:** Quattro Fontanili, graves FF 16–17 (**b, c**), GG 14–15 (**d**), FF 14–15 (**e**), CC 17 A (**f**).

Table 6. *Analysis of painted vases from Quattro Fontanili graves*

| Phase | Veii (QF) Grave | Vase-form | *Notizie degli Scavi* | Analysis Style | Clay |
|-------|-----------------|-----------|----------------------|-------|------|
| IIA | FF 16–17 | chevron skyphos Fig. 34b | 1963, 271 fig. 132b | Cycladic | Eretrian |
| | | chevron skyphos Fig. 34c | 1963, 271 fig. 132a | Veientine | Rogue: 'Western' |
| (?)IIA | EE 14–15 | chevron skyphos | 1965, 93 fig. 27 | Eretrian | Veientine |
| (?)IIA | CC 17 A | one-bird skyphos Fig. 34f | 1963, 149 fig. 47 | Eretrian | Eretrian |
| IIA/IIB | Z AA 7 | chevron skyphos | 1967, 222 fig. 81 | Eretrian | 'Western': ?Campanian |
| IIB | GG 14–15 | chevron skyphos Fig. 34d | 1965, 114 fig. 40 | Eretrian | Eretrian |
| IIB | FF 14–15 | chevron skyphos (associated with Fig. 34e) | 1965, 108 fig. 36h | Eretrian | Veientine |
| IIB | GG 16–17 | chevron skyphos | 1963, 192 fig. 76c | Veientine | 'Western': ?Campanian |
| IIB | GG HH 10 | olpe* | 1965, 188 fig. 89b | Veientine | Veientine |
| IIB | II 9–10 | mug* | 1965, 213 fig. 102 | Veientine | Eretrian |
| IIC | HH 10–11 | skyphos | 1965, 197 fig. 96 | Eretrian | Not clear |
| IIC | HH 6–7 | lekane* | 1967, 253 fig. 101 | Veientine | Veientine |
| IIC | GG 6–7 | small jug | 1967, 245 fig. 96 | Attic | 'Western': ?Campanian |

*Sources*: Phases: Toms 1986. Analyses: Descoeudres and Kearsley 1983 (style); Deriu et al. 1985 (clay; Mössbauer).

imported Euboean potter in Southern Etruria, based either at Veii or within striking distance, capable of preparing and using the local clay and of teaching others to do the same. This reading of the evidence is actually supported by the discrepancies between the Greek and Italian provenances derived from the analyses of style and of clay. The case of the two chevron skyphoi from the topographically adjacent graves EE 14–15 and FF 14–15 (see Table 6) is particularly striking in this respect. They are defined by Descoeudres, surely rightly, as 'almost certainly by the same potter' (Descoeudres and Kearsley 1983, 32), while the clay is defined by Mössbauer analysis as Veientine. We might well deduce that 'the skill and precision of the drawing and the exact reproduction of Greek designs and shapes point to Greek workmanship' (Blakeway 1933, 192) – which in these two cases we can, with Descoeudres, identify as Eretrian. In other words, before (probably not long before, but before) the middle of the eighth century, at least one expatriate Euboean potter seems to have been working in a Villanovan context in Southern Etruria exactly as he would have done at home. In a very real sense he was a precursor (and presumably not the only one) of the expatriate Corinthian aryballos specialists identified by C. W. Neeft at Pithekoussai sixty or seventy years later (ch. 4.4).

There is food for thought, too, in the fact that two vases made by the same immigrant potter were almost certainly deposited in two Quattro Fontanili graves of different periods: EE 14–15 is 'probably [still] IIA' (Toms 1986, 73–7), while FF 14–15 undoubtedly belongs to the succeeding IIB phase. This should remind us forcibly that the phases in the Toms

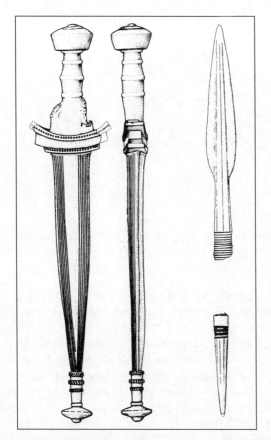

**Fig. 35.** Veii: Quattro Fontanili Villanovan cemetery. Weapons from grave AA1 (*Notizie degli Scavi* 1970, 296ff., figs. 79, 82; Toms 1986, phase IIB). Iron sword with bone and ivory hilt and bronze sheath; bronze spearhead and butt. Associated with the pieces illustrated in Figs. 36 and 37.

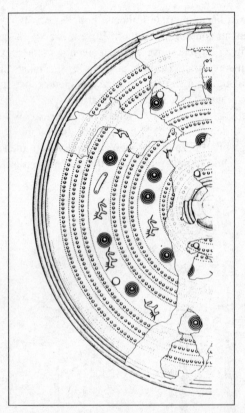

**Fig. 36.** Veii: Quattro Fontanili Villanovan cemetery. Bronze shield with embossed decoration, from grave AA1. Associated with the pieces illustrated in Figs. 35 and 37 (*Notizie* cit., fig. 77).

seriation are based exclusively on the incidence of 175 Villanovan artefact types in 225 Villanovan graves. They are thus, and not surprisingly, *Villanovan* phases, and *not* phases in the importation, imitation and deposition in Villanovan graves of Greek pottery. Indeed, whether we prefer the findings of stylistic analysis or of clay analysis, the Greek and Greek-type Geometric pottery in the Quattro Fontanili assemblage simply does not respect the internal divisions perceived for sound typological reasons in the Villanovan material: we have instead an alien 'chevron skyphos horizon' that literally spans the local IIA and IIB phases established by Toms. In other words, the first chevron skyphoi were deposited at Quattro Fontanili at the end of IIA, and it seems excessive to see them as representing a Euboean origin for the momentous innovations associated with that phase: notably the large scale use of iron (Fig. 35) and a dramatic increase in the number of bronze types

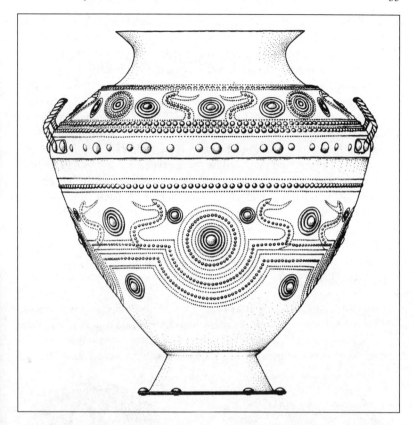

**Fig. 37.** Veii: Quattro Fontanili Villanovan cemetery. Sheet-bronze ossuary with embossed decoration, from grave AA1. Associated with the pieces illustrated in Figs. 35 and 36 (*Notizie* cit., fig. 72).

(including the introduction of sheet bronze: Figs. 36, 37) and in the number of actual examples of each type. True, Quattro Fontanili has yielded two skyphoi of the supposedly earlier Euboean type with pendent concentric semicircles (Kearsley 1989, 67f. nos. 229, 230; ch. 2.3 with Fig. 4) familiar in Cyprus and the Near East and joined in 1990 by an example from Sardinia (Bafico 1991), but they both belong to the latest type in R. Kearsley's new classification (Kearsley 1989, 142), and cannot be regarded as significantly earlier than the chevron skyphoi. All told, the ceramic aspects of the initial Euboean contacts with the West add their own weight to the proposal advanced in chapter 2.4 above: that the Euboeans were attracted by Etruscan metal resources that were already being exploited by others. The role of the indigenous Iron Age population in the process should not be underestimated: purely native interactions, some of them effected over long distances, are exemplified by the close relationship that linked Veii and Bologna from the end of the ninth century (Berardinetti Insam 1990, 12).

It should be noted, too, that early exchanges between outsiders and natives were not limited to fine pottery. Faience figurines and scarabs occur in phase IIA at Veii and in contemporary contexts elsewhere (for example at Cumae); of five or six seals of the Lyre-Player Group found in Etruria (Buchner and Boardman 1966, 25f. nos. 40–3*bis*; possibly Boardman 1990b, 12 no. 40*bis*), one from Falerii can be paralleled exactly at Pithe-koussai (Fig. 38), which may also be the source of the trinkets in some of the Quattro Fontanili graves defined in the previous section of this chapter as those of a nascent social élite. At Pithekoussai itself, reference has already been made to two miniature amphoras of fine impasto with incised double spirals found in graves of Late Geometric I and II (Fig. 13; ch. 4.4); their origin is to be sought in Southern Etruria or Latium vetus, where a member of the same class is associated in tomb xv at Castel di Decima with three Thapsos cups and an Early Protocorinthian globular aryballos (*CLP* 260–7 with pls. 63B-D, 65B).

Meanwhile, the arrival in Italy of imported Euboean potters was respon-sible for flourishing local productions not only of more or less close imita-tions of Euboean chevron skyphoi but also of painted versions in fine clay and heavily slipped impasto of wholly indigenous vase-forms. By the

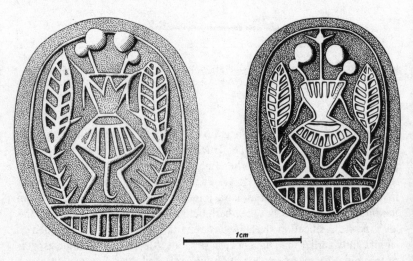

**Fig. 38.** Lyre-Player Group seals. *Left*: Pithekoussai, Valle di San Montano cemetery, 688–6 (Late Geometric I; Buchner and Boardman 1966, no. 5). *Right*: Falerii Veteres, Montarano cemetery, grave 17 (Buchner and Boardman 1966, no. 43). See also Fig. 15.

middle of the eighth century, we have every reason to think of local pottery workshops active within the Campanian spheres of the Capua and Ponte-cagnano groups and in the Valle del Sarno, in the mainstream and inland centres of Southern Etruria, and in Latium vetus. Throughout, there is a distinctly pre-colonial flavour to this production of local painted vases: it draws on the stylistic repertoire that was current in Greece before the appearance of the Corinthian Late Geometric Aetos 666 kotyle, the earliest Greek ceramic type extensively represented at Pithekoussai (Pl. 6, top left; ch. 4.4). In human terms, it is surely possible that when some Euboeans felt that the time was ripe to put down roots at Pithekoussai, others – including potters – had already established themselves (perhaps by intermarriage) in the native communities of the mainland. If so, it is only to be expected that the ceramic record of those communities owes more, quantitatively speak-ing, to the output of locally resident aliens and their pupils than it does to actual exchanges with or via Pithekoussai. Imported Thapsos cups and kraters, Early Protocorinthian kotylai and globular aryballoi and *Kreis-und Wellenbandstil* aryballoi are indeed present on some of the native Iron Age sites in Campania, at Castel di Decima and Satricum in Latium vetus (good selection of illustrations in *CLP*) and at Tarquinia, Caere and their territo-ries in Southern Etruria – but in quantities that can only be described as exiguous when compared with the superabundance of these types at con-temporary Pithekoussai or even with the relative frequency on the main-land, especially at Veii, of the earlier Euboean skyphos types (which are extremely rare at Pithekoussai: Fig. 21). In addition, the presence of even a few foreign artisans in widely separated native communities could have favoured not only interactions between the Campanian groups but also longer range cultural contact of the kind that distinguished the Bisenzio of the eighth century from its retarded predecessor of the ninth and its newly isolated successor of the seventh.

Finally, it is legitimate to ask what the first Greeks in the West were able to offer the early Etruscans in exchange for access to the mineral resources of Northern Etruria (where Geometric pottery of Euboean type is con-spicuous by its absence). The skyphoi and trinkets at Veii and elsewhere do not amount to a realistic answer to this question, although they are of course useful as trace elements of the underlying processes. Perhaps we should think in terms not so much of goods as of services: reference has been made above to the presence of resident alien potters and their pupils, and a similar model could no doubt be extended to other specialized crafts too. Metal-working is a prime example of a sphere in which the quality and quantity of production increases with a rapidity that clearly owes much to expertise that was not local: there are parallels at Pithekoussai for many of the fibula types that are now being produced on the mainland. A similar explanation, though involving a Phoenician stimulus, has been offered for the sudden burgeoning in the eighth century of advanced bronze technology at the Oenotrian centre of Francavilla Marittima in Calabria (ch. 6.2).

Interestingly enough, the question 'What had Greece to offer in return?' has also been asked and answered at the other end of the Mediterranean: 'The greatest gift to Cyprus from the Aegean ... was the diffusion of the Homeric poems in the late eighth century, which inspired the people of Salamis and Paphos to honour their rulers with a manner of burial which recalled in detail the funeral rites already immortalized in the Homeric poems' (Coldstream 1972, 22). Could not the Nestor kotyle, the Ajax and Achilles seal impression and aspects of the burial rite at Pithekoussai have equally momentous implications for the circulation of the Homeric poems in the West?

# 8    Etruscan epilogue

The decades that culminated in the rise and fall of Euboean Pithekoussai have been defined as the 'first really busy period' of East–West traffic (Boardman 1990a, 179). There is a lot to be said for this, although we should not underestimate the earlier feats of human ingenuity (and endurance) that achieved the degree of international physical standardization represented by the Late Bronze Age distribution of ox-hide ingots over the vast area between the Levant and Sardinia. Nevertheless, both in the Bronze Age and in the Iron Age, it is only too clear that the evidence of archaeology alone affords a very selective impression of what actually happened. Artefacts, even from assemblages as richly endowed and well excavated as those at Pithekoussai, cannot give us much more than half the story, and may indeed give us rather less. In the preceding chapters, I have been able to write woefully little about the *ideas* that were exported, exchanged, imitated and modified on a no less prodigious scale than Cypriot or Cypriot-type Bronze Age metal-work in Sardinia and Greek or Greek-type Geometric pottery around the Bay of Naples.

Occasionally, however, I have been able to invoke the discoveries made in adjacent fields of enquiry. Epigraphy is a case in point: some of the primary inscriptions on the amphora used *c.* 740 in the Pithekoussan *enchytrismos* grave 575 have been reliably identified as Semitic, and so too has the funerary symbol that can only refer to the secondary function of the vessel in the cemetery (Fig. 29). If these inscriptions suggest, as I believe they do, a Levantine origin for at least one of the parents of the baby inhumed in grave 575, there is further food for thought about contemporary commercial exchanges in the metrological indication of the Greek identity of the '200 [standard] units' (specified in one of the primary Semitic inscriptions) that the amphora was designed to contain. By the same token, if Phoenician craftsmen were really weighing out precious metals in the industrial quarter of Pithekoussai before the end of the eighth century, the only actual weight discovered there strongly suggests that they were operating on the Euboean standard. And the fact that the Greek inscription on the Nestor kotyle is Euboean provides a no less welcome identification of the place where the writer learnt his letters (Fig. 9).

Even in the early centuries with which this book has been concerned, the testimony of ancient authors is of at least some use, and the archaeology we have reviewed can sometimes improve its interpretation. Given the wide variety of geographical sources represented by the imported artefacts assigned to the Late Geometric I period in the Valle di San Montano cemetery at Pithekoussai, to say nothing of the massive influx of Early Protocorinthian characteristic of Late Geometric II (Figs. 18–20), I do not believe that the methods available to text-free archaeologists would have identified Pithekoussai as a Euboean foundation. Fortunately for history, Strabo and Livy were at hand: and in return no one should ever again translate *chruseia* at Strabo 5.4.9 as 'gold-mines'. On a wider front, the evidence for Levantine residents at Pithekoussai has shed new light on Odysseus' potentially disastrous relationship with a Phoenician at *Odyssey* 14.305–13: modern readers, like ancient listeners, can now appreciate that such dealings were common enough to provide a swindler with a plausible cover story. A similar view has been taken of another Homeric episode. When Athena decided to give Telemachus an unobtrusive helping hand in his search for his father (*Odyssey* 1.184), she appeared in the guise of a certain Mentes, who happened to be passing Ithaca on the wine-dark sea with a cargo of iron to exchange for copper. Her choice suggests that such men, and such trips, were commonplace enough not to attract undue attention (Snodgrass 1989, 29f.).

Best of all, the nature of the inscription on the Nestor kotyle for once brings us into contact with authentic, though anonymous, human activity. Without it, we might be tempted to suppose that Pithekoussai was 'inhabited not by human beings – stinking likeable witless intelligent incalculable real awful *people* – but by the pale phantoms of modern theory, who do not live, but just cower in ecological niches, get caught in catchment areas, and are entangled in redistributive systems' (Piggott 1985, 146). More often than not, however, the evidence for the first stage of Western Greek history lends itself to interpretative methods that are familiar to the prehistorian rather than to the historian. The same might well be said of the Etruscans, who in a very real sense inherited the international role of the Euboeans.

The momentous events on the island of Ischia, imperfectly perceived and briefly reviewed in the central part of this book, ended with the sudden diminution of the Euboeans' presence in both the East and the West at the end of the eighth century. Nevertheless, their impact on the native communities of the Italian mainland continued to be felt throughout the seventh century. Predictably, local schools of painted pottery were soon established (Williams 1986); Pithekoussan reminiscences abound in the so-called Cumano–Etruscan class at Tarquinia (Canciani 1974) and in the heron class widely exported from Caere and Veii (Leach 1987). The Etruscans, no doubt with some assistance, adopted the Euboean alphabet around 700, modifying it to the special needs of the phonetic systems that were already characteristic of the various geographical areas of the land between the Tiber and the Arno. Early in the seventh century and perhaps more visibly, the orientalizing princely (or 'heroic'?) tombs of Campania, Latium vetus and Etruria bear mute but magnificent witness to the absorption by the three native Iron Age entities defined in the last chapter of the formidable cargo of advanced techniques and connections placed before them by craftsmen who could no longer count on finding a Western niche at Pithekoussai. Their availability to serve the aspirations of the indigenous élites clearly gives rise to phenomena that recall some of those that we have seen at earlier stages in our story: above all, the difficulty (already apparent in the fine metal-work of Late Bronze Age Sardinia) of distinguishing the work of immigrant craftsmen from that of their native pupils – which also means, incidentally, that the significance of the master–apprentice relationship is already well established in the communities of the indigenous mainland, and henceforth amounts to the basis for the patient disentangling of 'hands', 'groups' and 'circles'. The human figure comes to the fore in orientalizing art, whether in Greek mythological scenes painted on vases (e.g. Coldstream 1968b) or incised on prestigious vessels like the gilded silver bowl from the Bernardini Tomb at Praeneste illustrated in Pl. 14: its narrative scenes of soldiers marching, country life and hunting are an anthology of aristocratic concerns; and its medley of stylistic affinities is matched by the mingling of Syrian, Cypriot, Cycladic and East Greek motifs visible in the decoration incised on an early seventh-century ostrich egg in the Tarquinia Museum (Torelli 1965).

The events of the eighth century resulted in many such combinations in the seventh, in society no less than art. From an early stage, Etruscan texts (none of which can be classed as literature or history) do at least reveal the existence of individuals with names. Some of them, like Larth Telicles and Rutile Hipucrates, are clearly of mixed Etruscan–Greek extraction – perhaps as a result of personal circumstances like those that lay behind the Phoenician funerary symbol employed on the amphora 575–1 in the Euboean cemetery at Pithekoussai. Greek vase shapes first seen in the West at Pithekoussai, notably Protocorinthian kotylai and aryballoi, are reproduced in bucchero (the only wholly original Etruscan product: Rasmussen 1979). Some of the Etruscan names for them, and occasionally for their contents, are no less clearly derived from Greek: Larth Telicles was the

**Pl. 14.** Palestrina (Praeneste, Latium vetus): gilded silver bowl from the orientalizing Bernardini Tomb.

proud possessor of a bucchero aryballos, defined by its inscription as a lekythos (*lechtumuza*; see Colonna 1974b for further examples).

Not all the seventh-century craftsmen operating in the orientalizing milieux on the Italian mainland were Greek, half Greek, of Greek extraction, or natives trained by members of any of these categories. Long before the full impact of eighth-century Pithekoussai on the seventh-century orientalizing scene was realized, it seemed appropriate to attribute at least some of the luxury items of gold, silver and especially ivory in the princely tombs of the mainland to craftsmen who stood in a similar relationship to the Levant (Brown 1960, 1–2). In both the Greek and the Levantine cases, there is every reason to think in terms of literal 'guest working'. This is, for example, the best definition that can be applied to certain seventh-century monumental stone sculptures at Caere and Bologna attributed with good reason to Syrian craftsmen who worked in wholly different ways in the two areas (Colonna and von Hase 1986): seated human figures carved in high relief on the walls of the Tomb of the Statues (*c.* 690–670) at Ceri in the territory of Caere; and local sandstone *stelai* (grave-markers) carved in low relief with elaborate vegetal forms in the environs of Bologna. It is difficult to avoid the conclusion that, from an early stage in the seventh century, sculptors were among the foreign craftsmen who could accept specific commissions north and south of the Apennines. But how did their indigenous patrons know what they wanted? Monumental sculpture is, after all, a sector in which Pithekoussai (where there is no stone worth carving) cannot be credited with setting a trend. And yet it is surely not a coincidence that in the eighth century both Caere (indeed Ceri itself) and Bologna have yielded typological straws in the wind that suggest a receptive atmosphere to direct contact in the seventh with areas – like Syria – which had long enjoyed fruitful connections with Euboea and its first Western base. At Ceri, tomb II in the Casaletti tumulus contained more items than any other *corredo* in Etruria that would be at home in the latest graves of the Late Geometric II period at Pithekoussai (Colonna 1968); at Bologna, a globular aryballos deposited (presumably as an heirloom) in a fifth-century grave in the Certosa cemetery has been recognized as a product of one of the expatriate Corinthian specialists who operated at Pithekoussai (Neeft 1987, 64: Potter/Painter Z, no. 5).

All told, it is not unreasonable to infer that the international character of eighth-century Pithekoussai spread, doubtless with changes of emphasis and additional elements, to the mainland centres in the early years of the seventh century. It provides an appropriate context in which, prior to his expulsion from Corinth and consequent emigration to Tarquinia in 657, Demaratus could become 'possessed of great wealth' (Dionysius of Halicarnassus 3.46.3–5) by trading with 'the cities of Tyrrhenia'. As for the consequences for Etruscan art and society of the events symbolized in the ancient written sources by Demaratus' emigration, suffice it to say here that they speak volumes for interaction between equals, or at the very least between two sides that had a great deal to give each other. As D. Musti (1987) has well shown, however, Demaratus' own claim to fame resides very largely in the only 'fact' about him reported in the earliest authority who mentions him (Polybius 6.11a.7): he was the Corinthian father of Lucius Tarquinius Priscus, the first Etruscan king of Rome (who reigned there between the traditional dates 616 and 579). As such, Demaratus' place in history was assured, and his story could be embroidered. If it was felt appropriate that Lucius should reach Rome as both rich (*divitiis potens*: Livy 1.34.1) and the son of a foreigner, the components of a suitable father figure could soon be assembled from the traditions of Corinthian entrepreneurial flair in the West generated by Corinthian commercial activities at Pithekoussai and subsequently on the mainland. There too, we may note that the vast quantities of seventh-century architectural terracottas afford clear evidence for the transformation of comparatively flimsy and frequently renewed huts into more permanent houses. This is an unmistakable sign of the transition from village to city, and in most cases to city-state: a development that was reached in Italy (outside Magna Graecia) only by Etruria, whence it passed first (with Lucius) to the Rome of the Tarquins and finally played a major part in the shaping of Western civilization as a whole.

The alphabet, the human figure in narrative art, the city-state idea: all of these reached Europe from Etruria. How they did so is a subject that is large enough for another book; happily, it already exists (Bonfante 1981). That Etruria possessed and was able to transmit these and other great gifts across the Alps is due in no small measure to the activities of the anonymous Euboean pioneers who came to the Far West and, by the middle of the eighth century, chose an island base for the operations that were to have a profound effect on the native peoples of the mainland and far beyond.

# Notes on further reading

## Chapter 1 Mycenaean prologue

### 1  The Mycenaeans in the West

The pace of comparatively recent Mycenaean discovery in the West can be gauged by comparing the catalogues of two exhibitions held in Taranto: Tiné and Vagnetti 1967 and, fifteen years later, Vagnetti 1982; unless otherwise indicated, material from the individual sites mentioned in the text of this section will be found in the latter item. See too the following general surveys: Vagnetti 1970 and 1980; Marazzi 1976; Marazzi and Tusa 1976 and 1979; Ridgway 1982a, 82–3; Harding 1984, 244–61. The proceedings of a major conference held in 1984 at Palermo (*Traffici micenei*) contain a wealth of factual information; discussion of wider issues will be found both there and in various papers in the proceedings of the 1984 Cambridge conference on Italian archaeology (*PIA* IV-3: especially Bergonzi 1985; Bietti Sestieri 1985). All future assessments of the Mycenaean material in the West, extant and yet to be found, will have to take account of Bietti Sestieri's (1988) brave attempt to construct 'a model in which the potential for inference is linked explicitly to the specific characteristics of the archaeological record'. See too Kilian 1990.

### 2  Italy at the beginning of the Iron Age

A fuller account of the matters treated in this section will be found in Ridgway 1988b, 623–33, which owes much to a brilliant synthesis by R. Peroni (1979b; see too Peroni 1980a and 1983). The fundamental achievements of the Italian school of artefact typology are enshrined in the Italian volumes, so far limited to the peninsula, in the Munich *PBF* series (e.g. Carancini 1975; Bianco Peroni 1970, 1979); see too the illustrated terminological dictionary (G. Bartoloni et al. 1980) and the collective volume on the Italian Final Bronze Age (Peroni 1980b) to which they have given rise; I have discussed these developments in two reviews (Ridgway 1978 and 1981b). Culturally, the Italian Final Bronze Age corresponds to the phenomenon known as Protovillanovan. I do not agree that this term is 'a rag-bag' (Harding 1984, 318): a more appropriate definition will be found in Fugazzola Delpino 1979 and Rittatore Vonwiller 1975, which is extensively illustrated.

## Chapter 2 The Euboeans at home and abroad

### *1 Introduction*

The title of this book is a deliberate reference to that of T. J. Dunbabin's pioneer synthesis (1948) of Western Greek affairs that was largely written before the Second World War; he achieved the union of historical and archaeological evidence advocated in three classic papers by his Oxford teacher A. Blakeway (1933, 1935, 1936). When Dunbabin died in 1955, he was working on a corresponding account of the relationship between Greece and the Near East in the Geometric and Archaic periods; Dunbabin 1957 preserves the lecture notes out of which it would have grown. Although Blakeway and Dunbabin were writing well before the effective discovery first of Pithekoussai (Buchner 1954a,b) and later of (Geometric) Euboea itself, there is a good deal of useful information in these items. The achievement of J. Bérard 1957 and 1960 is different and complementary: his central thesis that the historical colonists were familiar with the Western exploits of their legendary counterparts ensures that there is much of permanent value on the literary side of his work. Summary archaeological accounts of Euboean enterprise that take account of work at Pithekoussai and in Euboea will be found in Coldstream 1977 (see too his 1968a and 1983b,c for the specifically ceramic aspects), Boardman 1980 and – for historians – the relevant chapters of Murray 1980. Inevitably, conferences abound in this fast developing field, and so too (with varying degrees of time-lag) do their proceedings. The following are particularly valuable sources: *Contribution* (Naples 1972–3; published 1975); *CGICM* (Naples 1976; 1982); *Atti XVIII Taranto* (1978; 1984); *GIS* I–II (Athens 1979; 1983–4); *Nouvelle contribution* (Naples 1980; 1981); *Renaissance* (Athens 1981; 1983); *GCNP* (Sydney 1985; 1990). Finally, I have reviewed elsewhere the exegetical fortunes of the first Western Greeks over the last fifty years in more detail than is possible or appropriate here (Ridgway 1990a,b).

### *2 The Euboeans at home*

The 'modern period' of Euboean studies began with two papers on its pottery: Boardman 1952 and 1957 (see also his 1969). Further information on the three main sites mentioned in the text will be found in the following items: Chalcis: Bakhuizen 1975, 1976 and 1981; Mele 1981 (metallurgy); Andreiomenou 1984–7 (Geometric pottery). Eretria: Auberson and Schefold 1972 (guide to the excavations); Mele 1975 (early society); Andreiomenou 1976–85 (Eretrian Geometric and Subgeometric pottery) and 1985–6 (Attic Middle Geometric pottery from Eretria). Lefkandi: Popham and Sackett 1979 and 1980 (respectively plates and text: excavation report); Snodgrass 1983, 167–9 (demography: but see Popham 1990, 35 note 9); Popham et al. 1982b, 1989 (further excavation of the Toumba cemetery); Catling and Lemos 1990 (the pottery from the Protogeometric heroon). There is much of interest, too, in an unusually frank exchange of views between a recent Sather Lecturer (Snodgrass 1987) and the excavator of Lefkandi (Popham 1990). Hero cults: Coldstream 1976; C. Bérard 1982; Snodgrass 1982, 1988 (and cf. Whitley 1988). My account of the Lelantine War is based on Murray 1980, 76–9;

see also d'Agostino 1967 and, on Thucydides 1.15.3, Ste Croix 1972, 219 note 21 (I am grateful to P. A. Cartledge for this reference).

## 3 The Euboeans abroad

The typological classification and absolute chronology of Euboean pendent semi-circle skyphoi have been reviewed in depth by R. A. Kearsley 1989. The distribution of her first five successive but overlapping Types illustrates the steady progress of Euboean maritime trade from the Greek mainland and islands to Cyprus and the Levant (maps: Kearsley 1989, 134–8, figs. 45–7) and finally to the West (Type 6: Kearsley 1989, 139, fig. 48) – one from Villasmundo in eastern Sicily, and two from the Villanovan cemetery of Quattro Fontanili at Veii in Southern Etruria (Kearsley 1989, 67–70, cat. nos. 229, 230, 237). I am most grateful to Dr Kearsley for advising me that the pendent semicircle skyphos discovered in the 1990 excavation of the nuragic village at Sant'Imbenia near Alghero in Sardinia (Bafico 1991) appears to have more in common with certain Cypriot examples of her Type 5 than it does with her Type 6. The Euboean fragments from Al Mina include many pieces closely matched in the West (e.g. Robertson 1940, 3, fig. 1); see too Boardman 1958, 1965 (chronology), Popham 1980 (the Euboean connection), Descoeudres 1978 (Euboean imitations of Corinthian kotylai) and in general Boardman 1990a (see next section). Greeks and Phoenicians in the Aegean and in the Levant: Coldstream 1982 and Riis 1982 (these two items can conveniently be read in conjunction with Buchner 1982b), and more recently Niemeyer 1990. The best treatment of the Phoenicians in general is now Gras et al. 1989.

## 4 Sardinia

I have prepared two elementary guides to the extensive bibliography generated by the current boom in discovery and exegesis in Sardinia: Ridgway 1980, now rather out of date; and Ridgway 1989, which concentrates on Sardinia's role in episodes hitherto regarded as the exclusive preserve of Aegean specialists. Elsewhere, and prior to the discoveries at Sant'Imbenia briefly mentioned in the previous section, I have felt able to summarize my view of the relevance of Sardinia to the story of the first Western Greeks as follows: '[the] first chapter of Western Greek history should be read as the last chapter in a long story of contact between the Cypro-Levantine world and Sardinia that was in full working order throughout the period between the beginning of the Greek Dark Age and the despatch of the first Euboean pendent semicircle skyphoi to the East' (Ridgway 1990a, 69). A very different approach has subsequently been adopted by Sir John Boardman, who argues strongly against any 'important' continuity of East–West contacts prior to the 'first really busy period' of such traffic in the eighth century (Boardman 1990a). Given the extensive and long-lasting practical application of Cypriot metallurgical techniques in Sardinia (Lo Schiavo et al. 1985), it seems excessive to exclude the island from the Cypro-Levantine world-view around 1050. Relevant long-distance trade in the Mediterranean has been authoritatively reviewed by L. Vagnetti and F. Lo Schiavo (1989), and more evidence for it has since come to light. A bronze *obelos* (revolving spit) in the tenth/ninth century Monte Sa Idda hoard in Sardinia is matched by a specimen from a funerary context, assigned to the later part of Cypro-Geometric I, *c.* 1000 or soon after, at Amathus in Cyprus; these are the only non-Atlantic find-spots in the distribution of a Portuguese type (Karageorghis and Lo Schiavo 1989). No less surprising, and indicative, is the pottery askos from multiple tomb 2 (*c.* 850–680) at Khaniale Tekke in Crete, best known for its 'crocks of gold' – jewellery supposed by some to have been made by a Phoenician goldsmith; this allegedly mysterious item, first published as long ago as 1954, has at last been recognized as a characteristically Sardinian product (Vagnetti 1989). Nor is it without interest that ox-hide copper ingots, current in Sardinia between the fifteenth century and 900 (Lo Schiavo et al. 1990, 14–40), now appear – on the evidence of metallographic, elemental and statistical analyses – to derive from a single non-Sardinian source of raw material (Lo Schiavo et al. 1990, 203). Whether or not that source is in fact Cyprus, as has been suggested, is still *sub iudice*: for the moment, it is enough to stress that the ox-hide shape is notoriously international (Sandars 1985, 100–1, 210), and so too were the pressures that extended and maintained this degree of physical standardization from the Levant to Sardinia long before Boardman's 'first really busy period' of East–West traffic (Niemeyer 1984, 10 fig. 5; see further Ridgway 1991, and the references there cited).

For Euboean and Euboeanizing Geometric pottery at Sulcis, see the Notes to ch. 5.3.

## Chapter 3 Pithekoussai: an introduction

### *1 Sources and etymology*

The ancient references to Pithekoussai, Inarime and Aenaria are collected in Pauly–Wissowa, *Real-Encyclopädie* s.v. Aenaria (1893) and in Kleine Pauly s.v. Pithekusa (1972). The etymology of these names is discussed at length by Pais 1908b, 181–203, the English translation of a remarkably prophetic description (Pais 1900 = 1908a, 226–55) of the role of Pithekoussai in the early history of Magna Graecia: 'Even more than by the beauty of land and sky, and the excellence of the waters, the Chalcidians and Eretrians were probably attracted by the commercial opportunities which Ischia offered' (Pais 1908b, 183). Hence, perhaps, the cautious acceptance in the English-speaking world twenty years later of the island of Ischia – rather than Ischia da Castro near Etruscan Vulci – as the possible provenance for a stray Corinthian vase in an Irish private collection ('there is no reason why Greek burials should not exist there': Purser 1927, 36).

The account in the text owes much to an unpublished thesis (Buchner 1938); see too Ridgway 1973, 21–3 and, on Strabo's methods and priorities, the collections of papers edited by F. Prontera (1984) and G. Maddoli (1986). A primarily agricultural basis for the foundation (R. M. Cook 1962) cannot now be sustained.

### *2 Identification, excavation and configuration*

On Ischia generally (all periods, including vulcanology and the therapeutic properties of the waters) see: Buchner and Rittmann 1948; numerous contributions in *Atti Ischia*; and Monti 1980. The correspondence between Orsi, Spinazzola and Paribeni is preserved in the archive of the Archaeological Superintendency, Naples; the passages translated above are quoted by Buchner in the prefatory section of *Pithe-koussai I*, which also contains a summary of current views on Ischia's geomorphology, earthquakes and eruptions (ancient and modern; reviewed at greater length in Buchner 1986). The very different history of excavation and discovery at Cumae is discussed by Buchner 1977; here too, the role of Paolo Orsi (in charge of the Naples Superintendency 1900–1; Leighton 1986) was crucial in encouraging excavation (Pellegrini 1903; Karo 1904) and securing the acquisition and (probably) the publication of the material excavated 1878–84 and 1886–93 by E. Stevens (Gabrici 1913).

## Chapter 4 Pithekoussai: the cemetery in the Valle di San Montano

The information in this chapter is almost all derived from the 493 Late Geometric I and II graves excavated by Giorgio Buchner between 1952 and 1961. The forthcoming definitive publication of these campaigns, *Pithekoussai I*, has been preceded by a number of general accounts of the excavation and the finds in Italian (Buchner 1954a, 1961, 1964, 1969, 1973, 1983, 1985) and in English (Stoop 1955, Buchner 1966, Ridgway 1973); sections 2, 3 and 5 of this chapter also owe much to a set of studies of the burial rites, their combination in family plots and the evidence thus provided for social organization (Buchner 1975, 1982a; Ridgway 1982b, whence the statistical material and histograms in the text of section 5 of this chapter). More detailed treatments of the individual artefacts and artefact categories discussed in this chapter are listed below in the order of their appearance in the text of section 4; an analytical index of the pottery, with bibliography, from the *Pithe-koussai I* graves will be found in Ridgway 1982b, 76–99.

*The Nestor kotyle (168–9)*:  the vast specialist bibliography generated so far by this famous piece is collected by O. Vox in *Pithekoussai I* (Appendix I). Here it is sufficient to note the *editio princeps* (Buchner and Russo 1955), the principal *corpora* (Jeffery 1961, 235–6; Guarducci 1967, 226–7; Hansen 1983, no. 454, where the dates of manufacture and deposition are unfortunately misprinted as '535–520' and '525–520' – 200 years too late), and the latest treatments known to me (Risch 1987, Jourdan-Hemmerdinger 1988); B. B. Powell, *Homer and the origin of the Greek alphabet* (Cambridge 1991) is highly relevant, but reached me too late for consideration here. On the archaeological evidence for eighth-century literacy at Pithekoussai and elsewhere see Johnston 1983. Like Hansen 1976, I believe that the Pithekoussai verses contain a humorous suggestion, appropriate to the presumably convivial atmosphere associated with *symposia* (see Rathje 1990 for the wider cultural implications of Homeric banquets in the West).

The kotyle itself belongs to the first phase of the Rhodian Bird-kotyle Workshop defined by Coldstream (1968a, 277); its find circumstances are described in a successful rebuttal (Metzger 1965) of an eccentric attempt to lower the chronology of the inscription (Carpenter 1963). Two small fragments of a similar Rhodian kotyle from a Late Geometric non-funerary context at Eretria bear a total of eighteen letters from a three-line (and apparently hexametric) inscription; the first line may be a statement of ownership by one Thymokares/Thymokrates (Johnston and Andreiomenou 1989).

See chapter 6.3 on the possible Levantine origin of the family plot in which grave 168 occurs.

*The Pithekoussai Shipwreck (Sp 1/1):*    the detailed description that will eventually appear in *Pithekoussai I* has been published in English (Ridgway 1988c, 97–8); the 'new' drawing (Fig. 10) first appeared in Buchner 1966, and differs crucially from that published in the *editio princeps* (Buchner 1954b, 42 fig. 1; it later became clear that the feature initially interpreted as a tall central mast is simply one of ten vertical struts with a swastika in the field above). The reading of the scene as a narrative was first proposed by S. Brunnsåker (1962). See also Morrison and Williams 1968, 34 (Geom. 32); Ermeti 1976; and, on Geometric figured scenes generally, Snodgrass 1980.

Kreis- und Wellenbandstil *aryballoi:*    on the type see Johansen 1958, 155–61. The case for expatriate Phoenician manufacture at Ialysos is well made by Coldstream 1969.

*Levantine aryballoi:*    these are the earliest aryballoi of any kind in the West, where they are so far confined to the eight examples in five Late Geometric I graves (of which three cremations and one inhumation survive) forthcoming in *Pithekoussai I*. Like the *Kreis- und Wellenbandstil* aryballoi of Late Geometric II, this type also finds its closest parallels in Rhodes: Blinkenberg 1931, col. 300 s.v. 'Vases à parfums du $3^e$ type' (Lindos); Johansen 1958, 161–4 (Exochi). The North Syrian face aryballos from a Late Geometric II cremation grave (and hence heavily burnt; 215–4) is also unique in the West. The face comes from the same mould as the examples from Zinjirli (von Luschan and Andrae 1943, 47 fig. 48) and Tarsus (Goldman et al. 1963, 333–40, fig. 155 no. 21). For the possible significance of Levantine aryballoi as ethnic indicators, see chapter 6.3.

*Early Protocorinthian globular aryballoi:*    a complete classification of the category has been prepared by C. W. Neeft (1987), who was fortunately able to take account of all the specimens found at Pithekoussai. His globular aryballos period begins ten years later (715) than the conventional date adopted here for the beginning of the Late Geometric II period (725), and ends later too (between 680 and 670 rather than 700: Neeft 1987, 380, 307). Expatriate Corinthian workshops at Pithekoussai: Neeft 1987, 59–65, 309 with 306 fig. 180 and 312 fig. 181.

*Local aryballoi and lekythoi:*    the category has been successively defined as Cretan (at Cumae), Euboean and finally 'Made in Ischia': see text, chapter 5.3.

*Argive Monochrome:*    uniquely among the categories of mass-produced and widely distributed eighth-century Greek ceramic exports, the small and unpretentious conical lekythoi of this type are made by hand. N. Kourou has made the interesting suggestion that they were associated with a particular substance: 'a kind of drug, perhaps opium, that could be used [either] as an offering to a vegetation goddess or as a sedative for a suffering person, and consequently accompanying him or her in the last journey to the underworld' (cf. Homeric *nepenthes, Odyssey* 4.221: Kourou 1988, 322; see too Kourou 1987).

*Thapsos cups, Corinthian Late Geometric (Aetos 666) and Early Protocorinthian kotylai:* the *Pithekoussai I* examples of these categories are included in Neeft's classifications: Neeft 1981 (the Thapsos class; see also Grimanis et al. 1980 and Dehl 1982); Neeft 1975 (kotylai).

Due account is also taken of the *Pithekoussai I* representatives of all the Early Protocorinthian categories in other major treatments of this most elegant of the Greek eighth-century fabrics: Benson 1986, 1989; Dehl 1984, summarized 1986.

*Euboean imitations of Protocorinthian kotylai:* Buchner 1964, 268 with fig. 1c,d; cf. Boardman 1959 and Descoeudres 1978 for Greek potters at Al Mina.

*Amphoras:* F. Durando has conducted a fascinating metrological investigation of all the amphoras in *Pithekoussai I* (Durando 1989): see the text of chapter 6.3 for his findings concerning Pithekoussai 575–1. The Attic SOS type: Johnston and Jones 1978.

*'Anforette' from the Italian mainland:* on this native type, the treatment of T. Dohrn (1965) has been superseded by that of A. Beijer (1978). 944–4 (Late Geometric I; from the second series of excavations in the Valle di San Montano; Buchner and Ridgway 1983) belongs to Beijer's Type 1a; 159–3 (Late Geometric II; Fig. 13) belongs to his Type 1b.

*Scarabs:* the numerous scarabs and other *aegyptiaca* from the first series of excavations in the Valle di San Montano cemetery are treated in depth by F. De Salvia in *Pithekoussai I* (Appendix II). They have previously been discussed in S. Bosticco's (1957) pioneer study, G. Hölbl's corpus (1979; see too Hölbl 1983) and by De Salvia himself (1975, 1978, 1983). The chronological implications of the Bocchoris scarab (325–16) at Pithekoussai were first discussed by R. M. Cook (1969); on the Calabrian askos 325–4 associated with it, see de La Genière 1968, 104, 240; on the Bocchoris vase at Tarquinia and its context, see Hencken 1968, 364–78 with fig. 361g and Rathje 1979, 150–2.

*Lyre-Player Group seals:* the known examples of this attractive category have been collected and reviewed by Buchner and Boardman 1966 (which includes virtually all those in *Pithekoussai I*) and Boardman 1990b; the grand total now stands at 187, of which rather more than half were found in the Pithekoussai cemetery. On the inscribed seal from Francavilla Marittima, see Guzzo Amadasi 1977 and Boardman 1990b, 6f. ('I am not convinced that the seal is inscribed at all').

*Personal ornaments:* a full typological classification of the bronze fibulas in South Italy, including all the *Pithekoussai I* specimens, is at an advanced stage of active preparation by F. Lo Schiavo (*PBF* XIV-8); for some of the issues raised see meanwhile Kilian 1973.

## Chapter 5 Pithekoussai: the non-funerary sites

*1–2   Monte di Vico and Mezzavia*

The two excavations described in this chapter were carried out in 1965 (the acropolis dump on Monte di Vico) and between 1969 and 1971 (the suburban industrial complex in the Mezzavia locality). After those dates, there are numerous references to both sites in the general accounts of work at Pithekoussai cited at the beginning of the Notes to chapter 4; see in addition Buchner 1971 and Klein 1972 (both in English), where virtually all the individual pieces mentioned in chapter 5 are presented and illustrated. The East Greek, Attic S O S, Massaliot, Etruscan, Phoenicio-Punic and local amphoras from Monte di Vico have been published by N. Di Sandro (1986; and see P. Bartoloni 1987 for useful further comments on the Phoenicio-Punic and unidentified pieces). Only a few additional comments need be made here, in the order suggested by the text. Euboean Middle Geometric chevron skyphoi: the fragments from Monte di Vico are discussed in Ridgway 1981a. On the occurrence of the same type in mainland Campania and Etruria, see chapter 7.2 and the references there cited. The 'unusual local piece' (*Pithekoussai 1*, Sp. 4/4): Ridgway 1981a, 48f. note 18 with 57 fig. 1. Iron-working: the artefacts defined as '*tuyères* (bellows mouthpieces)' in the text have been studied in a fascinating paper by S. P. Morris (1985), who provides an extensive catalogue of examples from Greece, Cyprus, Crete, the Black Sea, Italy, Sicily, France and Spain. She equates the type with *lasana*, devices used (seemingly in pairs) to support cooking pots in ancient Greek kitchens at home and abroad. There is a lot to be said in favour of this hypothesis; and although I have opted for the Scottish verdict of 'not proven' as far as the Pithekoussai specimens (S. P. Morris 1985, 406) are concerned, I would certainly not feel able to postulate metallurgical activity on the Pithekoussan acropolis in the absence of any other indication. But the slag – two substantial crates of it – and crucibles also encountered on Monte di Vico imply the existence of at least one forge there at some stage (probably after the demise of the Mazzola site); and as well as resembling the ancient illustrations of terracotta pot props collected by Professor Morris, the examples from Pithekoussai also resemble that of a *tuyère* in full working order on an Attic black figure kantharos from the Athenian acropolis (Hartwig 1896, 369 with pl. 7). It remains true, of course, that the slag, crucibles and '*tuyères*' are not demonstrably associated; and that the Monte di Vico assemblage has yielded abundant evidence in most periods for eating and drinking. On balance, I conclude that the metal-workers of Pithekoussai had hearty appetites.

*3   Conclusions*

Local aryballoi and lekythoi (see also ch. 4): Payne's Cretan definition (1931) of the Cumaean representatives of these two categories of small funerary vases was accepted by Blakeway (1933, 202; 1935, 130, 134) and Dunbabin (1948, 4). Euboeanizing urn and lid from Sulcis: Coldstream 1968a, 388, 429; Tronchetti 1979; Ridgway 1986, 179–80. As noted in chapter 2.4, Sulcis has yielded a handful of Euboean and Euboeanizing Geometric sherds (P. Bartoloni et al. 1988) and a second Euboean(izing) lid similar to that associated with the urn (P. Bartoloni 1989, 170 fig. 2) – for which a close parallel has also emerged, nearly forty years after its discovery, at Caere in Southern Etruria (Rizzo 1989, 29–38). Iberian fibula: the battered example *a doble resorte* at Pithekoussai (Lo Schiavo 1978, 40) may come from a tomb dismantled in the circumstances described in chapter 4.3: it was found in the fill of an undiagnostic inhumation grave, Pithekoussai 700, of (probably) Late Geometric II date. Its Sardinian parallel comes from a votive accumulation in the Grotta Pirosu, Su Benatzu (Santadi, prov. Cagliari: Lo Schiavo 1978, 39; Ridgway 1986, 181 fig. 7). Phoenician merchantmen in Spain: see in general Boardman 1990a (cf. ch. 2.4) and Niemeyer 1984, 1990.

### Chapter 6 Pithekoussai: status and function

Section 1 of this chapter is a modified version of passages that first appeared in Ridgway 1981a, 53–6. The ideas in sections 2 and 3 were first expounded in 1978 at the XVIII Convegno di Studi sulla Magna Grecia, Taranto and eventually published in its *Atti* (Ridgway 1984b). With the single exception indicated below, further references to the individual artefacts and categories mentioned in the text will be found in the Notes to chapter 4.4 or in the captions to the relevant illustrations. I make no comment here on the thesis of M. Bernal concerning what he sees as the excessive promotion of Greece at the expense of the Semitic component in Greek civilization: for the purposes of this book, I do not consider that Bernal 1987 supersedes Albright 1941.

*The Semitic inscriptions on the amphora* Pithekoussai 1, *575–1*: Buchner 1978; Garbini 1978; Johnston 1983, 63f.; Guzzo Amadasi 1987, 23 no. 10. The writing has also been read as Phoenician (Teixidor 1979, 387 no. 137), and F. M. Cross has compared the script to that used *c.* 800 on the Kition Bowl from Cyprus (Ridgway 1986, 178f.); my impression is that the initial Aramaic identification is preferred by the majority of those better qualified to judge than I am. The other Semitic inscriptions mentioned in the text of section 3 are briefly assessed in the items by Buchner, Johnston and Guzzo Amadasi cited above.

### Chapter 7 Campania, Latium vetus and Southern Etruria in the ninth and eighth centuries

#### 1 The native context

In addition to the items cited in the text of this brief *tour d'horizon* of the indigenous Iron Age, the following works are indispensable: Campania: de La Genière 1979; Johannowsky 1983; *Napoli antica*; d'Agostino and Gastaldi 1988. For the history of discovery at Cumae, see Buchner 1977 and the Notes to chapter 3.2. Latium vetus: Colonna 1974c; *CLP* (extensively illustrated); Ridgway 1979; Cornell 1980, 1986. Southern Etruria: Colonna 1975; Fugazzola Delpino 1984; Ridgway 1988b, 640–53; G. Bartoloni 1989. Excavation reports on the Villanovan cemetery of Quattro Fontanili at Veii have been published in *Notizie degli Scavi* (1963, 77–279; 1965, 49–236; 1967, 87–286; 1970, 178–329; 1972, 195–384; 1975, 63–184; 1976, 149–220) and discussed by Close-Brooks and Ridgway 1979,

95–113; Toms 1986; Berardinetti Insam 1990. Other Villanovan cemeteries: Hencken 1968 and Buranelli 1983 (Tarquinia); Delpino 1977 (Bisenzio).

### 2   The first contacts with the Euboeans

I have written at greater length elsewhere on the lines followed in this section (Ridgway 1988a), the subject-matter of which is well covered by G. Bartoloni 1989, 175–207 and Delpino 1990; see too Rizzo 1989.

## Chapter 8 Etruscan epilogue

In this *envoi*, I have attempted to estimate the long-term impact of the first Western Greeks on the most significant and familiar native inhabitants of pre-Roman Italy (Ridgway 1988b, 653–75). An adequate bibliography of the Etruscans themselves and their civilization would be at least as long again as that assembled at the end of this book. Fortunately, the 300 or so most important items (excluding journal articles) published between 1978 and 1990 have been accessibly listed and introduced by my wife: Serra Ridgway 1991. I have treated the Demaratus story at greater length than is possible here in the Jerome Lectures that I was privileged to deliver in Ann Arbor and Rome during the academic year 1990–1; the published version is in preparation (Ridgway forthcoming).

# Abbreviations

Many of the following abbreviations for collective works, conference proceedings and a few other items have been used in the text and Notes on further reading; nearly all of them reappear, with some additions, in the Bibliography.

| | |
|---|---|
| *Atti Ischia* | *Atti del Centro Studi sull'isola d'Ischia: ricerche, contributi e memorie 1944–1970*. Naples, 1971 |
| *Atti XVIII Taranto* | *Gli Eubei in Occidente* (Atti del XVIII° Convegno di Studi sulla Magna Grecia, Taranto 1978). Taranto, 1984 |
| *CGICM* | *La céramique grecque ou de tradition grecque au VIIIᵉ siècle en Italie centrale et méridionale* (Cahiers du Centre Jean Bérard 3). Naples, 1982 |
| *CIL* | *Corpus Inscriptionum Latinarum*. Berlin, 1863 onwards |
| *CLP* | *Civiltà del Lazio primitivo* (exhibition catalogue). Rome, 1976 |
| *Contribution* | *Contribution à l'étude de la société et de la colonisation eubéennes* (Cahiers du Centre Jean Bérard 2). Naples, 1975 |
| *FGrHist* | F. Jacoby, *Fragmente der griechischen Historiker*. Berlin, 1926–58 |
| *GCNP* | J.-P. Descoeudres (ed.), *Greek colonists and native populations* (Proceedings of the First Australian Congress of Classical Archaeology, held in honour of Emeritus Professor A. D. Trendall, Sydney 1985). Canberra/Oxford, 1990 |
| *GIS I–II* | *Atti del Convegno Internazionale* 'Grecia, Italia e Sicilia nell'VIII e VII secolo a.C.', *Atene 1979*. Vol. I: *Annuario della Scuola Archeologica di Atene* 59 (1981[1983]). Vol. II: ibid. 60 (1982[1984]) |
| *IBR* | D. and F. R. Ridgway (eds.), *Italy before the Romans: the Iron Age, orientalizing and Etruscan periods*. London/New York/San Francisco, 1979 |
| *MM* | G. Gnoli and J.-P. Vernant (eds.), *La mort, les morts dans les sociétés anciennes*. Cambridge, 1982 |
| *Napoli antica* | *Napoli antica* (exhibition catalogue; Soprintendenza |

archeologica per le provincie di Napoli e Caserta).
Naples, 1985

*Nouvelle contribution*    *Nouvelle contribution à l'étude de la société et de la colonisation eubéennes* (Cahiers du Centre Jean Bérard 6). Naples, 1981

*PBF*    H. Müller-Karpe (ed.), *Prähistorische Bronzefunde*. Munich, 1969 onwards

*PCIA*    *Popoli e civiltà dell'Italia antica*, I-IX. Rome, 1974–89

*PIA IV-3*    C. Malone and S. Stoddart (eds.), *Papers in Italian archaeology IV: the Cambridge conference 1984, 3. Patterns in protohistory* (British Archaeological Reports, International Series 245). Oxford, 1985

*Pithekoussai I*    G. Buchner and D. Ridgway, *Pithekoussai I: La necropoli. Tombe 1–723 scavate dal 1952 al 1961* (Monumenti Antichi, new series 4). Rome, in press

*PIW*    H. G. Niemeyer (ed.), *Phönizier im Westen* (Beiträge des Internationalen Symposiums in Köln, 1979; Madrider Beiträge 8). Mainz, 1982

*Renaissance*    R. Hägg (ed.), *The Greek Renaissance of the eighth century BC: tradition and innovation* (Proceedings of the Second International Symposium at the Swedish Institute in Athens, 1981). Stockholm, 1983

*SSA III*    M. S. Balmuth (ed.), *Nuragic Sardinia and the Mycenaean world* (Studies in Sardinian Archaeology III; British Archaeological Reports, International Series 387). Oxford, 1987

*Traffici micenei*    M. Marazzi, S. Tusa and L. Vagnetti (eds.), *Traffici micenei nel Mediterraneo: problemi storici e documentazione archeologica* (Atti del Convegno di Palermo, 1984). Taranto, 1986

# Bibliography

Åkerström, Å. (1943) *Der Geometrische Stil in Italien* (Skrifter utgivna av Svenska Institutet i Rom 4°, 9). Lund

Albright, W. F. (1941) 'New light on the early history of Phoenician colonization', *Bulletin of the American Schools of Oriental Research* 83: 14–22

Andreiomenou, A. (1976–85) Series of five extensively illustrated papers (in Greek) on Geometric and Subgeometric pottery from Eretria: *Archaiologiké Ephemeris* 1975 [1976], 206–29; 1977 [1979], 128–63; 1981 [1983], 84–113; 1982 [1984], 161–86; 1983 [1985], 161–92

(1984–7) 'Skyphoi de l'atelier de Chalcis (fin xᵉ-fin vⅢᵉ s. av. J.-C.)', *Bulletin de Correspondance Hellénique* 108 (1984) 37–69 and 109 (1985) 49–75; see also 110 (1986) 89–120 and *Philia epe eis G. E. Mylonas* II, Athens 1987, 71–98

(1985–6) 'Keramik aus Eretria: Attisch-Mittelgeometrisch II', *Athenische Mitteilungen* 100 (1985) 23–38 and 101 (1986) 97–111

Andrewes, A. (1967) *The Greeks*. London

Angle, M. and Zarattini, A. (1987) 'L'insediamento protostorico di Casale Nuovo', *Archeologia Laziale* 8: 250–2

Auberson, P. (1975) 'Chalcis, Lefkandi, Erétrie au vⅢᵉ siècle', in *Contribution*, 9–14

Auberson, P. and Schefold, K. (1972) *Führer durch Eretria*. Bern

Austin, M. and Vidal-Naquet, P. (1972) *Economies et sociétés en Grèce ancienne*. 2nd edn, Paris

Bafico, S. (1991) 'Greci e Fenici ad Alghero', *Archeo* 74 (aprile), 18

Bailo Modesti, G. (1980) *Cairano nell'età arcaica* (Annali, Istituto Orientale, Napoli: Archeologia e Storia Antica, Quaderni 1). Naples

Bakhuizen, S. C. (1975) 'Iron and Chalcidian colonization in Italy', *Mededelingen van het Nederlands Instituut te Rome* 37: 15–26

(1976) *Chalcis-in-Euboea, iron and Chalcidians abroad* (Chalcidian Studies 3). Leiden

(1981) 'Le nom de Chalcis et la colonisation chalcidienne', in *Nouvelle Contribution*, 163–74

Bartoloni, G. (1989) *La cultura villanoviana: all'inizio della storia etrusca*. Rome

(1990) 'Veio nell'vⅢ secolo e le prime relazioni con l'ambiente greco', in *Atti II Congresso Internazionale Etrusco, Firenze 1985* I, 117–28. Rome

Bartoloni, G., Bietti Sestieri, A. M., Fugazzola Delpino, M. A., Morigi Govi, C., Parise Badoni, F. (1980) *Materiali dell'Età del Bronzo Finale e della prima Età del Ferro*. Florence (see Ridgway 1981b)

Bartoloni, P. (1987) Review of Di Sandro 1986. *Rivista di Studi Fenici* 15: 104–9
   (1989) 'Nuove testimonianze arcaiche da Sulcis', *Nuovo Bullettino Archeologico Sardo* 2 [1985]: 167–92
Bartoloni, P., Bernardini, P. and Tronchetti, C. (1988) 'S. Antioco: area del Cronicario (campagne di scavo 1983–86)', *Rivista di Studi Fenici* 16: 73–119
Bass, G. (1967) *Cape Gelidonya: a Bronze Age shipwreck* (Transactions of the American Philosophical Society, 57–8). Philadelphia
Beijer, A. (1978) 'Proposta per una suddivisione delle anfore a spirale', *Mededelingen van het Nederlands Instituut te Rome* 40: 7–21
Beloch, J. (1890) *Campanien*. 3rd edn, Breslau
Benson, J. L. (1986) 'An Early Protocorinthian workshop and the sources of its motifs', *Bulletin Antieke Beschaving* 61: 1–20
   (1989) *Earlier Corinthian workshops: a study of Corinthian Geometric and Protocorinthian stylistic groups*. (Allard Pierson series, Scripta Minora, 1). Amsterdam
Benton, S. (1953) 'Further excavations at Aetos', *Annual of the British School at Athens* 48: 255–361
Bérard, C. (1970) *L'Hérôon à la porte de l'ouest* (Eretria 3). Bern
   (1982) 'Récupérer la mort du prince: héroïsation et formation de la cité, in *MM*, 89–105
Bérard, J. (1957) *La colonisation grecque de l'Italie et de la Sicile dans l'antiquité: l'histoire et la légende*. 2nd edn, Paris
   (1960) *L'expansion et la colonisation grecques*. Paris
Berardinetti Insam, A. (1990) 'La fase iniziale della necropoli villanoviana di Quattro Fontanili. Rapporti con le comunità limitrofe', *Dialoghi di Archeologia* 8/1: 5–28
Bergonzi, G. (1985) 'Southern Italy and the Aegean during the Late Bronze Age: economic strategies and specialised craft products', in *PIA* IV-3, 355–87
Bernal, M. (1987) *Black Athena. The Afroasiatic roots of classical civilization, I: the fabrication of ancient Greece 1785–1985*. London/New Brunswick, NJ
Bianco Peroni, V. (1970) *Die Schwerter in Italien* (PBF IV-1). Munich
   (1979) *I rasoi nell'Italia continentale* (PBF VIII-2) (see Ridgway 1981b)
Bietti Sestieri, A. M. (1973) 'The metal industry of continental Italy, 13th–11th century, and its Aegean connections', *Proceedings of the Prehistoric Society* 39: 383–424
   (1985) 'Contact, exchange and conflict in the Italian Bronze Age: the Mycenaeans on the Tyrrhenian coasts and islands', in *PIA* IV-3, 305–37
   (1988) 'The "Mycenaean connection" and its impact on the central Mediterranean societies', *Dialoghi di Archeologia* 6/1: 23–51
Blakeway, A. (1933) 'Prolegomena to the study of Greek commerce with Italy, Sicily and France in the eighth and seventh centuries BC', *Annual of the British School at Athens* 33: 170–208
   (1935) ' "Demaratus": a study in some aspects of the earliest Hellenisation of Latium and Etruria', *Journal of Roman Studies* 25: 129–49
   (1936) 'The date of Archilochus', in *Greek poetry and life: essays presented to Gilbert Murray on his 70th birthday*, 34–55. Oxford
Blanco, A. and Luzón, J. M. (1969) 'Pre-Roman silver miners at Riotinto', *Antiquity* 43: 124–31

Blinkenberg, C. (1931) *Lindos* I. Berlin

Boardman, J. (1952) 'Pottery from Eretria', *Annual of the British School at Athens* 47: 1–48

(1957) 'Early Euboean pottery and history', *Annual of the British School at Athens* 52: 1–29

(1958) 'Al Mina and Greek chronology', *Historia* 7: 250

(1959) 'Greek potters at Al Mina?', *Anatolian Studies* 9: 163–9

(1965) 'Tarsus, Al Mina and Greek chronology', *Journal of Hellenic Studies* 85: 5–15

(1969) 'Euboean pottery in West and East', *Dialoghi di Archeologia* 3: 102–14

(1980) *The Greeks overseas: their early colonies and trade*. 3rd edn, London

(1990a) 'Al Mina and history', *Oxford Journal of Archaeology* 9: 169–90

(1990b) 'The Lyre-Player Group of seals: an encore', *Archäologischer Anzeiger*, 1–17

Bonfante, L. (1981) *Out of Etruria: Etruscan influence north and south* (British Archaeological Reports, International Series 103). Oxford

Bosticco, S. (1957) 'Scarabei egiziani della necropoli di Pithecusa nell'isola di Ischia', *Parola del Passato* 12: 215–29

Brown, W. L. (1960) *The Etruscan lion*. Oxford

Brunnsåker, S. (1962) 'The Pithecusan Shipwreck', *Opuscula Romana* 4: 165–242

Buchner, G. (1938) 'Vita e dimora umana nelle isole flegree dall'epoca preistorica ai tempi romani (Ischia, Procida, Vivara)'. Unpublished thesis, University of Rome

(1954a) 'Scavi nella necropoli di Pithecusa 1952–53', *Atti e Memorie della Società Magna Grecia* 1: 3–11

(1954b) 'Figürlich bemalte spätgeometrische Vasen aus Pithekussai und Kyme', *Römische Mitteilungen* 60–1: 37–55

(1961) s.v. 'Ischia', in *Enciclopedia dell'Arte Antica* IV, 224–9. Rome

(1964) Contribution to discussion, in *Metropoli e colonie di Magna Grecia* (Atti III Taranto 1963), 263–74

(1966) 'Pithekoussai: oldest Greek colony in the West', *Expedition* 8 (Summer): 4–12

(1969) 'Mostra degli scavi di Pithecusa', *Dialoghi di Archeologia* 3: 85–101

(1971) 'Recent work at Pithekoussai (Ischia), 1965–71', *Archaeological Reports for 1970–71*, 63–7

(1973) s.v. 'Ischia', in *Enciclopedia dell'Arte Antica, Supplemento 1970*, 376–9. Rome

(1975) 'Nuovi aspetti e problemi posti dagli scavi di Pithecusa con particolari considerazioni sulle oreficerie di stile orientalizzante antico', in *Contribution*, 59–86 (a translated and adapted version of part of this item appears as Buchner 1979)

(1977) 'Cuma nell'VIII secolo a.C., osservata dalla prospettiva di Pithecusa', in *I Campi Flegrei nell'archeologia e nella storia* (Atti dei convegni Lincei 33), 131–48

(1978) 'Testimonianze epigrafiche semitiche dell'VIII secolo a.C. a Pithekoussai', *Parola del Passato* 33: 135–47

(1979) 'Early orientalizing: aspects of the Euboean connection', in *IBR*, 129–44 (see Buchner 1975)

(1982a) 'Articolazione sociale, differenze di rituale e composizione dei corredi nella necropoli di Pithecusa', in *MM*, 275–87

(1982b) 'Die Beziehungen zwischen der euböischen Kolonie Pithekoussai auf der Insel Ischia und dem nordwestsemitischen Mittelmeerraum in der zweiten Hälfte des 8. Jhs. v. Chr.', in *PIW*, 277–306

(1983) 'Pithekoussai: alcuni aspetti peculiari', in *GIS* I, 263–73

(1985) 'L'*emporion* di Pithecusa', in *Napoli antica*, 79–87

(1986) 'Eruzioni vulcaniche e fenomeni vulcano-tettonici di età preistorica e storica nell'isola d'Ischia', in C. Albore Livadie (ed.), *Tremblements de terre, eruptions volcaniques et vie des hommes dans la Campanie antique* (Bibliothèque de l'Institut Français de Naples IIᵉ série, 7), 145–88. Naples

Buchner, G. and Boardman, J. (1966) 'Seals from Ischia and the Lyre-Player Group', *Jahrbuch des Deutschen Archäologischen Instituts* 81: 1–62

Buchner, G. and Ridgway, D. (1983) 'Pithekoussai 944', *Annali, Istituto Orientale, Napoli: Archeologia e Storia Antica* 5: 1–9

Buchner, G. and Rittmann, A. (1948) *Origine e passato dell'isola d'Ischia*. Naples

Buchner, G. and Russo, C. F. (1955) 'La coppa di Nestore e un'iscrizione metrica da Pithecusa dell'VIII secolo av. Cr.', *Rendiconti Lincei* 10: 215–34

Buchner Niola, D. (1965) *L'isola d'Ischia: studio geografico* (Memorie di geografia economica e antropica 3). Naples

Buranelli, F. (1983) *La necropoli villanoviana 'Le Rose' di Tarquinia* (Quaderni del Centro di Studio per l'Archeologia Etrusco-Italica 6). Rome

Canciani, F. (1974) *Corpus Vasorum Antiquorum: Tarquinia, Museo Archeologico Nazionale* III. Rome (see Ridgway 1977)

Carancini, G. L. (1975) *Die Nadeln in Italien* (PBF XIII-2) (see Ridgway 1978)

Carpenter, R. (1963) Review of Jeffery 1961, *American Journal of Philology* 84: 76–85

Casaubon, I. (1587) *Strabonis rerum geographicarum libri xvii*. Geneva

Catling, R. W. V. and Lemos, I. S. (1990) *Lefkandi II: The Protogeometric Building at Toumba, I. The Pottery*. London

Chevalley de Rivaz, J. E. (1835) *Description des eaux minéro-thermales et des étuves de l'île d'Ischia*. 2nd edn, Naples

Childe, V. G. (1960) 'The Italian axe-mould from Mycenae', in *Civiltà del Ferro*, 575–8. Bologna

Close-Brooks, J. and Ridgway, D. (1979) 'Veii in the Iron Age', in *IBR*, 95–127 (originally published in Italian: *Notizie degli Scavi* (1965) 53–64 and *Studi Etruschi* 35 (1967) 323–9 (Close-Brooks: phases and chronology); *Studi Etruschi* 35 (1967) 311–21 (Ridgway: skyphoi))

Coldstream, J. N. (1968a) *Greek Geometric pottery*. London

(1968b) 'A figured Geometric oinochoe from Italy', *Bulletin of the Institute of Classical Studies* 15: 86–96

(1969) 'The Phoenicians of Ialysos', *Bulletin of the Institute of Classical Studies* 16: 1–8

(1971) 'The Cesnola Painter: a change of address', *Bulletin of the Institute of Classical Studies* 18: 1–15

(1972) 'Cypro-Aegean exchanges in the ninth and eighth centuries BC', in *Praktika tou protou Diethnou Kyprologikou Synedriou* A 1, 15–22. Nicosia

(1976) 'Hero-cults in the age of Homer', *Journal of Hellenic Studies* 96: 8–17
(1977) *Geometric Greece*. London
(1982) 'Greeks and Phoenicians in the Aegean', in *PIW*, 261–75
(1983a) 'Gift exchange in the eighth century BC', in *Renaissance*, 201–7
(1983b) 'Some problems of eighth-century pottery in the West, seen from the Greek angle', in *CGICM*, 21–37 (and see also ibid. 216–21: 'bilan archéologique')
(1983c) 'The meaning of the regional styles in the eighth century BC', in *Renaissance*, 17–25
Colonna, G. (1968) s.v. 'Caere', *Studi Etruschi* 36: 265–71
(1973) 'Ricerche sull'Etruria interna volsiniese', *Studi Etruschi* 41: 45–72
(1974a) 'Ceramica geometrica dell'Italia meridionale nell'area etrusca', in *Aspetti e problemi dell'Etruria interna* (Atti VIII Convegno Nazionale Studi Etruschi, Orvieto 1972), 297–302
(1974b) 'Nomi etruschi di vasi', *Archeologia Classica* 25–6: 132–50
(1974c) 'Preistoria e protostoria di Roma e del Lazio', in *PCIA* II, 275–346
(1975) 'Basi conoscitive per una storia economica dell'Etruria', in *Supplemento, Annali 22 dell'Istituto Italiano di Numismatica*, 3–23
Colonna, G. and von Hase, F.-W. (1986) 'Alle origini della statuaria etrusca: la Tomba delle Statue presso Ceri', *Studi Etruschi* 52: 13–59
Cook, J. M. et al. (1959) 'Old Smyrna, 1948–1951', *Annual of the British School at Athens* 53–4: 1–181
Cook, R. M. (1962) 'Reasons for the foundation of Ischia and Cumae', *Historia* 11: 113–14
(1969) 'A note on the absolute chronology of the 8th and 7th centuries BC', *Annual of the British School at Athens* 64: 13–15
Cornell, T. J. (1980) 'Rome and Latium vetus, 1974–79', *Archaeological Reports for 1979–80*, 71–89
(1986) 'Rome and Latium vetus, 1980–86', *Archaeological Reports for 1985–86*, 123–33
Cross, F. M. (1972) 'An interpretation of the Nora Stone', *Bulletin of the American Schools of Oriental Research* 208: 13–19
d'Agostino, B. (1967) 'Osservazioni a proposito della guerra lelantina', *Dialoghi di Archeologia* 1: 20–37
(1974) 'La civiltà del ferro nell'Italia meridionale', in *PCIA* II, 11–91
(1979) 'Le necropoli protostoriche della Valle del Sarno: la ceramica di tipo greco', *Annali, Istituto Orientale, Napoli: Archeologia e Storia Antica* 1: 59–75
d'Agostino, B. and Gastaldi, P. (1988) *Pontecagnano II: La necropoli del Picentino, 1. Le tombe della prima età del ferro* (Annali, Istituto Orientale, Napoli: Archeologia e Storia Antica, Quaderni 5). Naples
D'Andria, F. (1984) 'Il Salento nell'VIII e VII sec. a.C.: nuovi dati archeologici', in *GIS* II, 101–16
De Caro, S. (1986) *Saggi nell'area del tempio di Apollo a Pompei: saggi stratigrafici di A. Maiuri nel 1931–32 e 1942–43* (Annali, Istituto Orientale, Napoli: Archeologia e Storia Antica, Quaderni 3). Naples
Dehl, C. (1982) 'Zur Herkunft der Thapsosklasse', in *Praestant Interna. Festschrift für U. Hausmann*, 182–9. Tübingen

162     *Bibliography*

(1984) *Die korinthische Keramik des 8. und frühen 7. Jhs. v. Chr. in Italien: Untersuchungen zu ihrer Chronologie und Ausbreitung.* Berlin

(1986) 'Cronologia e diffusione della ceramica corinzia dell'VIII sec. a.C. in Italia', *Archeologia Classica* 35: 186–210

de La Genière, J. (1968) *Recherches sur l'âge du fer en Italie méridionale: Sala Consilina* (Bibliothèque de l'Institut Français de Naples IIᵉ série, 1). Naples

(1979) 'The Iron Age in Southern Italy', in *IBR*, 59–93

Delpino, F. (1977) 'La prima età del ferro a Bisenzio: aspetti della cultura villanoviana nell'Etruria meridionale interna', *Memorie Lincei* 21: 453–93

(1990) 'L'ellenizzazione dell'Etruria villanoviana: sui rapporti tra Grecia ed Etruria fra IX e VIII secolo a.C.', in *Atti II Congresso Internazionale Etrusco, Firenze 1985* I, 105–16. Rome

Deriu, A., Boitani, F. and Ridgway, D. (1985) 'Provenance and firing techniques of Geometric pottery from Veii: a Mössbauer investigation', *Annual of the British School at Athens* 80: 139–50

Deriu, A., Buchner, G. and Ridgway, D. (1986) 'Provenance and firing techniques of Geometric pottery from Pithekoussai: a Mössbauer investigation', *Annali, Istituto Orientale, Napoli: Archeologia e Storia Antica* 8: 99–116

De Salvia, F. (1975) 'I reperti di tipo egizio di Pithekoussai: problemi e prospettive', in *Contribution*, 87–97

(1978) 'Un ruolo apotropaico dello scarabeo egizio nel contesto culturale grecoarcaico di Pithekoussai (Ischia)', in *Hommages à Maarten J. Vermaseren* III, 1003–61. Leiden

(1983) 'Un aspetto di *Mischkultur* ellenico-semitica a Pithekoussai (Ischia): i pendagli metallici del tipo a falce', in *Atti I Congresso Internazionale di Studi Fenici e Punici, Roma 1979* III, 89–95. Rome

Desborough, V. R. d'A. (1957) 'A group of vases from Amathus', *Journal of Hellenic Studies* 77: 212–19

(1976) 'The background to Euboean participation in early Greek maritime enterprise', in *Tribute to an Antiquary: essays presented to Marc Fitch by some of his friends*, 25–40. London

Descoeudres, J.-P. (1978) 'Euboeans in Australia: some observations on the imitations of Corinthian kotylai made in Eretria and found in Al Mina', in *Eretria* VI, 7–19. Bern

Descoeudres, J.-P. and Kearsley, R. (1983) 'Greek pottery at Veii: another look', *Annual of the British School at Athens* 78: 9–53

De Siano, F. (1801) *Brevi e succinte notizie di storia naturale e civile dell'isola d'Ischia.* Naples [1798]

De Simone, C. (1978) 'Un nuovo gentilizio etrusco di Orvieto (Katacina)', *Parola del Passato* 33: 370–95

Dickinson, O. T. P. K. (1986) 'Early Mycenaean Greece and the Mediterranean', in *Traffici micenei*, 271–6

Di Sandro, N. (1986) *Le anfore arcaiche dallo Scarico Gosetti, Pithecusa.* (Cahiers des amphores archaïques et classiques 2; Cahiers du Centre Jean Bérard 12). Naples (see P. Bartoloni 1987)

Dohrn, T. (1965) 'Die etruskische Bandhenkelamphora des 7. Jh. v. Chr.', in *Studi in onore di Luisa Banti*, 143–52. Roma

Douglas, N. (1931) *Summer islands.* London

Dunbabin, T. J. (1948) *The Western Greeks*. Oxford

(1957) *The Greeks and their Eastern neighbours*. London

Durando, F. (1989) 'Indagini metrologiche sulle anfore commerciali arcaiche della necropoli di Pithekoussai', *Annali, Istituto Orientale, Napoli: Archeologia e Storia Antica* 11: 55–120

Ermeti, A. L. (1976) 'La nave geometrica di Pithecusa', *Archeologia Classica* 28: 206–15

Falsone, G. (1978) 'Il simbolo di Tanit a Mozia e nella Sicilia punica', *Rivista di Studi Fenici* 6: 137–51

Frederiksen, M. W. (1977) 'Archaeology in South Italy and Sicily, 1973–76', *Archaeological Reports for 1976–77*, 43–76

(1979) 'The Etruscans in Campania', in *IBR*, 277–311

Fugazzola Delpino, M. A. (1976) *Testimonianze di cultura appenninica nel Lazio*. Florence

(1979) 'The Protovillanovan: a survey', in *IBR*, 31–51

(1984) *La cultura villanoviana. Guida ai materiali della prima età del ferro nel Museo di Villa Giulia*. Rome

Gabrici, E. (1913) *Cuma* (Monumenti Antichi 22). Rome

Garbini, G. (1978) 'Un'iscrizione aramaica a Ischia', *Parola del Passato* 33: 148–55

Gastaldi, P. (1979) 'Le necropoli protostoriche della Valle del Sarno: proposta per una suddivisione', *Annali, Istituto Orientale, Napoli: Archeologia e Storia Antica* 1: 13–57

Goldman, H., Hanfmann, G. M. A., Porada, E. (1963) *Excavations at Gozlu Kula, Tarsus III: the Iron Age*. Princeton

Graham, A. J. (1964) *Colony and mother city in ancient Greece*. Manchester

Gras, M. (1985) *Trafics tyrrhéniens archaïques* (Bibliothèques des Ecoles françaises d'Athènes et de Rome 258). Paris/Rome

Gras, M., Rouillard, P., Teixidor, J. (1989) *L'univers phénicien*. Paris

Grimanis, A. P., Filippakis, S. E., Perdikatsis, B., Vassiliki-Grimanis, M., Bosana-Kourou, N., Yalouris, N. (1980) 'Neutron activation and X-ray analysis of "Thapsos class" vases: an attempt to identify their origin', *Journal of Archaeological Science* 7: 227–39

Guarducci, M. (1964) 'Appunti di epigrafia arcaica', *Archeologia Classica* 16: 122–53

(1967) *Epigrafia Greca I*. Rome

Guzzo Amadasi, M. G. (1977) '[Francavilla Marittima.] Scarabeo siro-fenicio', *Atti e Memorie della Società Magna Grecia* 15–17: 60–4

(1987) 'Iscrizioni semitiche di nord-ovest in contesti greci e italici (X–VII sec. a.C.)', *Dialoghi di Archeologia* 5/2: 13–27

Hankey, V. (1952) 'Late Helladic tombs at Khalkis', *Annual of the British School at Athens* 47: 49–95

Hansen, P. A. (1976) 'Pithecusan humour: the interpretation of "Nestor's Cup" reconsidered', *Glotta* 54: 25–43

(1983) *Carmina epigraphica graeca saeculorum viii–v a Chr. n.* Berlin/New York

Harding, A. F. (1984) *The Mycenaeans and Europe*. London/Orlando FL

Hartwig, P. (1896) 'Une gigantomachie sur un canthare de l'acropole d'Athènes', *Bulletin de Correspondance Hellénique* 20: 364–73

Hencken, H. (1968) *Tarquinia, Villanovans and early Etruscans*. Cambridge, MA

Hill, G. F. (1899) *A handbook of Greek and Roman coins*. London

Hölbl, G. (1979) *Beziehungen der ägyptischen Kultur zu Altitalien*. Leiden
  (1983) 'Die Aegyptiaca des griechischen, italischen und westphönikischen Raumes aus der Zeit des Pharao Bocchoris (718/17–712 v. Chr.)', *Grazer Beiträge* 10: 1–20

Jeffery, L. H. (1961) *The local scripts of Archaic Greece*. Oxford (see Carpenter 1963)

Johannowsky, W. (1983) *Materiali di età arcaica della Campania*. Naples

Johansen, K. F. (1958) 'Exochi: ein frührhodisches Gräberfeld', *Acta Archaeologica* 28: 1–192

Johnston, A. W. (1983) 'The extent and use of literacy: the archaeological evidence', in *Renaissance*, 63–8

Johnston, A. W. and Andreiomenou, A. (1989) 'A Geometric graffito from Eretria', *Annual of the British School at Athens* 84: 217–20

Johnston, A. W. and Jones, R. E. (1978) 'The SOS amphora', *Annual of the British School at Athens* 73: 103–41

Jones, R. E. (1986) 'Chemical analysis of Aegean-type Late Bronze Age pottery found in Italy', in *Traffici micenei*, 205–14

Jones, R. E. and Day, P. M. (1987) 'Late Bronze Age Aegean and Cypriot-type pottery on Sardinia: identification of imports and local imitations by physicochemical analysis', in *SSA III*, 257–70

Jourdan-Hemmerdinger, D. (1988) 'L'epigramma di Pitecusa e la musica della Grecia antica', in B. Gentili and R. Pretagostini (eds.), *La musica in Grecia*, 145–82. Bari

Karageorghis, V. (1982) *Cyprus from the Stone Age to the Romans*. London

Karageorghis, V. and Lo Schiavo, F. (1989) 'A West Mediterranean obelos from Amathus', *Rivista di Studi Fenici* 17: 15–29

Karo, G. (1904) 'Tombe arcaiche di Cuma', *Bullettino di paletnologia italiana* 30: 1–29

Kearsley, R. (1989) *The pendent semicircle skyphos: a study of its development and chronology and an examination of it as evidence for Euboean activity at Al Mina* (Institute of Classical Studies, Bulletin Supplement 44). London

Kilian, K. (1973) 'Zum italischen und griechischen Fibelhandwerk des 8. und 7. Jahrhunderts', *Hamburger Beiträge zur Archäologie* 3: 1–39
  (1990) 'Mycenaean colonization: norm and variety', in *GCNP*, 445–67

Klein, J. J. (1972) 'A Greek metal-working quarter: eighth-century excavations on Ischia', *Expedition* 14 (Winter): 34–9

Kourou, N. (1987) 'A propos de quelques ateliers de céramique fine, non tournée du type "Argien Monochrome"', *Bulletin de Correspondance Hellénique* 111: 31–53
  (1988) 'Handmade pottery and trade: the case of the "Argive Monochrome" ware', in *Proceedings of the Third Symposium on ancient Greek and related pottery, Copenhagen 1987*, 314–24

Kurtz, D. C. and Boardman, J. (1971) *Greek burial customs*. London

Landi, A. (1976) 'L'etimo di *Epomeus* (Tim. ap. Strab. v 248)', *Rendiconti dell'Accademia di Archeologia, Lettere e Belle Arti, Napoli* 51: 39–52

Leach, S. S. (1987) *Subgeometric pottery from Southern Etruria* (Studies in Mediterranean archaeology and literature, Pocket book 54). Göteborg

Leighton, R. (1985) 'Evidence, extent and effects of Mycenaean contacts with south-east Sicily during the Late Bronze Age', in *PIA* IV-3, 399–412
(1986) 'Paolo Orsi (1859–1935) and the prehistory of Sicily', *Antiquity* 60: 15–20

Lepore, E. (1976) 'Timeo in Strabone v.4.3 C242–243 e le origini campane', in *Mélanges offerts à Jacques Heurgon*, 573–85. Paris

Lo Schiavo, F. (1978) 'Le fibule della Sardegna', *Studi Etruschi* 46: 25–46

Lo Schiavo, F., Macnamara, E. and Vagnetti, L. (1985) 'Late Cypriot imports to Italy and their influence on local bronzework', *Papers of the British School at Rome* 53: 1–71

Lo Schiavo, F., Maddin, R., Merkel, J., Muhly, J. D. and Stech, T. (1990) *Metallographic and statistical analyses of copper ingots from Sardinia* (Soprintendenza ai Beni Archeologici per le provincie di Sassari e Nuoro, Quaderni 17). Ozieri (see Ridgway 1991)

Lo Schiavo, F. and Ridgway, D. (1987) 'La Sardegna e il Mediterraneo allo scorcio del II millennio', in *La Sardegna nel Mediterraneo tra il secondo e il primo millennio a.C.* (Atti del 2º Convegno di ... Selargius, 1986), 391–418. Cagliari

Lo Schiavo, F. and Vagnetti, L. (1986) 'Frammento di vaso miceneo(?) da Pozzomaggiore (Sassari)', in *Traffici micenei*, 199–204

Lo Schiavo, F., Vagnetti, L. and Ferrarese Ceruti, M. L. (1980) 'Micenei in Sardegna?', *Rendiconti Lincei* 35: 371–93

Luce, J. V. (1976) 'Asteris and the twin harbours', *Journal of Hellenic Studies* 96: 157–9

Macnamara, E. (1970) 'A group of bronzes from Surbo, Italy: new evidence for Aegean contacts with Apulia during Mycenaean III B and C', *Proceedings of the Prehistoric Society* 36: 241–60

Macnamara, E., Ridgway, D. and Ridgway, F. R. (1984) *The bronze hoard from Santa Maria in Paùlis, Sardinia* (British Museum Occasional Paper 45). London

Macnamara, E. and Wilkes, W. G. St J. (1967) 'Underwater exploration of the ancient port of Nora, Sardinia', *Papers of the British School at Rome* 35: 4–11

Maddoli, G. (1986) ed., *Strabone: contributi allo studio della personalità e dell'opera* II. Perugia

Maggiani, A. (1973) 'Coppa fenicia da una tomba villanoviana di Vetulonia', *Studi Etruschi* 41: 73–95

Maiuri, A. (1930) 'Aspetti e problemi dell'archeologia campana', *Historia* [Milan] 4: 58–82

Marazzi, M. (1976) *Egeo e Occidente alla fine del II millennio a.C.* Rome

Marazzi, M. and Tusa, S. (1976) 'Interrelazioni dei centri siciliani e peninsulari durante la penetrazione micenea', *Sicilia Archeologica* 9: 49–90
(1979) 'Die mykenische Penetration im westlichen Mittelmeerraum', *Klio* 61: 309–51

Markoe, G. (1985) *Phoenician bronze and silver bowls from Cyprus and the Mediterranean* (University of California Classical Studies 26). Berkeley CA

Martín de la Cruz, J. C. (1988) 'Mykenische Keramik aus bronzezeitlichen Sied-
lungsschicten von Montoro am Guadalquivir', *Madrider Mitteilungen* 29:
77–92

McCarter, P. K. (1975) 'A Phoenician graffito from Pithekoussai', *American
Journal of Archaeology* 79: 140–1

Mele, A. (1975) 'I caratteri della società eretriese arcaica', in *Contribution*, 15–26
    (1979) *Il commercio greco arcaico: prexis ed emporie* (Cahiers du Centre Jean
    Bérard 4). Naples
    (1981) 'I Ciclopi, Calcodonte e la metallurgia calcidese', in *Nouvelle Contribu-
    tion*, 9–33

Metzger, H. (1965) 'Sur la date du graffite de la "coupe de Nestor"', *Revue des
Etudes Anciennes* 67: 301–5

Moeller, W. O. (1970) 'The riot of A D 59 at Pompeii', *Historia* 19: 84–95

Momigliano, A. (1963) 'An interim report on the origins of Rome', *Journal of
Roman Studies* 53: 95–121

Monti, P. (1980) *Ischia: archeologia e storia*. Naples

Morris, I. (1987) *Burial and ancient society: the rise of the Greek city-state.*
Cambridge

Morris, S. P. (1985) '*Lasana*: a contribution to the ancient Greek kitchen', *Hesperia*
54: 393–409

Morrison, J. S. and Williams, R. T. (1968) *Greek oared ships, 900–322 BC.* Cambridge.

Mountjoy, P. A. (1986) *Mycenaean decorated pottery: a guide to identification*
(Studies in Mediterranean Archaeology 73). Göteborg

Müller-Karpe, H. (1959) *Beiträge zur Chronologie der Urnenfelderzeit nördlich
und südlich der Alpen.* Berlin
    (1962) 'Zur spätbronzezeitlichen Bewaffnung in Mitteleuropa und Griechen-
    land', *Germania* 40: 255–87

Munz, F. R. (1970) 'Die Zahnfunde aus der griechischen Nekropole von Pithekoussai auf Ischia', *Archäologischer Anzeiger*, 452–75

Mureddu, P. (1972) '*Chruseia* a Pithekoussai', *Parola del Passato* 27: 407–9

Murray, O. (1980) *Early Greece.* London

Musti, D. (1987) 'Etruria e Lazio arcaico nella tradizione (Demarato, Tarquinio,
Mezenzio)', in *Etruria e Lazio arcaico* (Quaderni del Centro di Studio per
l'Archeologia Etrusco-Italica 15). Rome
    (1990) *Storia greca: linee di sviluppo dall'età micenea all'età romana.* 2nd edn,
    Rome/Bari

Neeft, C. W. (1975) 'Corinthian fragments from Argos at Utrecht and the Corinthian Late Geometric kotyle', *Bulletin Antieke Beschaving* 50: 97–134
    (1981) 'Observations on the Thapsos class', *Mélanges de l'Ecole Française de
    Rome, Antiquité* 93: 7–88
    (1987) *Protocorinthian Subgeometric aryballoi.* (Allard Pierson series 7).
    Amsterdam

Niemeyer, H. G. (1984) 'Die Phönizier und die Mittelmeerwelt im Zeitalter
Homers', *Jahrbuch des Römisch-Germanischen Zentralmuseums, Mainz* 31:
3–94
    (1990) 'The Phoenicians in the Mediterranean: a non-Greek model for expansion
    and settlement in antiquity', in *G C N P*, 469–89

Orton, C. R. and Hodson, F. R. (1981) 'Rank and class: interpreting the evidence from prehistoric cemeteries', in S. C. Humphreys and H. King (eds.), *Mortality and immortality: the anthropology and archaeology of death*, 103–15. London

Pais, E. (1900) 'Per la storia d'Ischia nell'antichità', *Rivista di Storia Antica* 5: 465–92

(1908a) *Ricerche storiche e geografiche sull'Italia antica*. Turin

(1908b) *Ancient Italy: historical and geographical investigations in central Italy, Magna Grecia, Sicily and Sardinia*. Chicago/London

Pallottino, M. (1951–3) 'Qualche annotazione in margine al CIE II, sect. I, fasc. I (Orvieto)', *Studi Etruschi* 21 (1950–1) 229–37 and 22 (1952–3) 179–95

(1978) *The Etruscans*. 2nd edn, Harmondsworth (originally published in Italian as *Etruscologia*, Milan 1973; revised 6th edn)

(1991) *A history of earliest Italy*. London (originally published in Italian as *Storia della prima Italia*, Milan 1984)

Payne, H. (1931) *Necrocorinthia*. Oxford

Pellegrini, G. (1903) 'Tombe greche arcaiche e tomba greco-sannitica a tholos della necropoli di Cuma', *Monumenti Antichi* 13: 201–96

Peroni, R. (1979a) 'Prime presenze micenee in Calabria', *Magna Grecia* 14, fasc. 11–12: 1–2

(1979b) 'From Bronze Age to Iron Age: economic, historical and social considerations', in *IBR* 7–30 (originally published in Italian: *Parola del Passato* 24 (1969) 134–60)

(1980a) 'Le prime popolazioni dell'età dei metalli', in L. Fasani (ed.), *Archeologia*, 139–70. Milan

(1980b) ed., *Il Bronzo Finale in Italia* (Archeologia, Materiali e Problemi 1). Bari (see Ridgway 1981b)

(1983) 'Presenze micenee e forme socio-economiche nell'Italia protostorica', in *Magna Grecia e mondo miceneo* (Atti XXII Taranto 1982), 211–84

Piggott, S. (1985) Review of T. Champion, C. Gamble, S. Shennan and A. Whittle, *Prehistoric Europe*, *Antiquity* 59: 145–6

Popham, M. (1980) 'Al Mina and Euboea', *Annual of the British School at Athens* 75: 151–61

(1983) 'Why Euboea?', in *GIS* I, 237–9

(1987) 'An early Euboean ship', *Oxford Journal of Archaeology* 6: 353–9

(1990) 'Reflections on *An Archaeology of Greece* [Snodgrass 1987]: surveys and excavation', *Oxford Journal of Archaeology* 9: 29–35

Popham, M. R., Calligas, P. G. and Sackett, L. H. (1989) 'Further excavation of the Toumba cemetery at Lefkandi, 1984 and 1986. A preliminary report', *Archaeological Reports for 1988–89*, 117–29

Popham, M. R., Sackett, L. H. and Themelis, P. G. (1979, 1980) *Lefkandi I: The Iron Age. The settlement; the cemeteries* (plates 1979; text 1980). London

Popham, M. R., Touloupa, E. and Sackett, L. H. (1982a) 'The hero of Lefkandi', *Antiquity* 56: 169–74

Popham, M. R., Touloupa, E. and Sackett, L. H. (1982b) 'Further excavation of the Toumba cemetery at Lefkandi, 1981', *Annual of the British School at Athens* 77: 213–48

Porada, E. (1956) 'A Lyre-Player from Tarsus and his relations', in *The Aegean and*

*the Near East: studies presented to Hetty Goldman*, 185–211. Locust Valley
NY

Prontera, F. (1984) ed., *Strabone: contributi allo studio della personalità e dell'opera* I. Perugia

Purser, O. (1927) 'Ancient pottery at Shanganagh Castle', *Proceedings of the Royal Irish Academy, Section C*, 37: 36–52

Randall-MacIver, D. (1927) *The Etruscans*. Oxford

Rasmussen, T. B. (1979) *Bucchero pottery from Southern Etruria*. Cambridge

Rathje, A. (1979) 'Oriental imports in Etruria in the eighth and seventh centuries
BC: their origins and implications', in *IBR*, 145–83

(1990) 'The adoption of the Homeric banquet in central Italy in the orientalizing
period', in O. Murray (ed.), *Sympotica: a symposium on the symposion*,
279–88. Oxford

Ridgway, D. (1973) 'The first Western Greeks: Campanian coasts and Southern
Etruria', in C. and S. Hawkes (eds.), *Greeks, Celts and Romans*, 5–38.
London

(1977) Review of Canciani 1974, *Archeologia Classica* 29: 218–23

(1978) Review of Carancini 1975, *Proceedings of the Prehistoric Society* 44:
468–70

(1979) 'Early Rome and Latium: an archaeological introduction', in *IBR*,
187–96

(1980) 'Archaeology in Sardinia and Etruria, 1974–79', *Archaeological Reports
for 1979–80*, 54–70

(1981a) 'The foundation of Pithekoussai', in *Nouvelle Contribution*, 45–56

(1981b) Review of Bianco Peroni 1979, G. Bartoloni et al. 1980 and Peroni
1980b, *Proceedings of the Prehistoric Society* 47: 342–4

(1982a) 'Archaeology in South Italy, 1977–81', *Archaeological Reports for
1981–82*, 63–83

(1982b) 'The eighth-century pottery at Pithekoussai: an interim report', in
*CGICM*, 69–101

(1984a) *L'alba della Magna Grecia* (Archeologia 7). Milan (the first edition of
the present work)

(1984b) 'Tra Oriente e Occidente: la Pithecusa degli Eubei', in *Atti XVIII Taranto*,
65–81

(1986) 'Sardinia and the first Western Greeks', in M. S. Balmuth (ed.), *Sardinia
in the Mediterranean* (Studies in Sardinian Archaeology II), 173–85. Ann
Arbor

(1988a) 'Western Geometric pottery: new light on interactions in Italy,' in *Proceedings of the Third Symposium on ancient Greek and related pottery,
Copenhagen 1987*, 489–505

(1988b) Ch. 12, 'Italy from the Bronze Age to the Iron Age', and Ch. 13, 'The
Etruscans', in *Cambridge Ancient History* IV, 623–75. 2nd edn, Cambridge

(1988c) 'The Pithekoussai shipwreck', in *Studies in honour of T. B. L. Webster* II,
97–107. Bristol

(1989) 'Archaeology in Sardinia and South Italy, 1983–88', *Archaeological
Reports for 1988–89*, 130–47

(1990a) 'The first Western Greeks and their neighbours 1935–1985', in *GCNP*,
61–72

(1990b) 'La "precolonizzazione" ', in *Un secolo di ricerche in Magna Grecia* (Atti XXVIII Taranto 1988), 111–26

(1991) 'Understanding oxhides' (review of Lo Schiavo et al. 1990), *Antiquity* 65: 420–2

(forthcoming) *Before Demaratus* (Thomas Spencer Jerome Lectures 27). Ann Arbor

Riis, P. J. (1970) *Sukas I: the north-east sanctuary and the first settling of Greeks in Syria and Palestine.* Copenhagen

(1982) 'Griechen in Phönizien', in *PIW*, 237–59

Risch, E. (1987) 'Zum Nestorbecher aus Ischia', *Zeitschrift für Papyrologie und Epigraphik* 70: 1–9

Rittatore Vonwiller, F. (1975) 'La cultura protovillanoviana', in *PCIA* IV, 11–60

Rizzo, M. A. (1989) 'Ceramica etrusco-geometrica da Caere', in *Miscellanea Ceretana* I (Quaderni del Centro di Studio per l'Archeologia Etrusco-Italica 17), 9–39. Rome

Robertson, C. M. (1940) 'Excavations at Al Mina, Sueidia: the early Greek vases', *Journal of Hellenic Studies* 60: 2–21

Rocco, B. (1970) 'Greco o fenicio?', *Sicilia Archeologica* 12: 5–7

Roebuck, C. (1972) 'Some aspects of urbanization in Corinth', *Hesperia* 41: 96–127

Sackett, L. H., Hankey, V., Howell, R. J., Jacobsen, T. W. and Popham, M. R. (1966) 'Prehistoric Euboea: contributions toward a survey', *Annual of the British School at Athens* 61: 33–112

Ste Croix, G. E. M. de (1972) *The origins of the Peloponnesian War.* London

Sandars, N. K. (1968) *Prehistoric art in Europe* (Pelican History of Art). Harmondsworth

(1985) *The Sea Peoples: warriors of the ancient Mediterranean, 1250–1150 BC.* 2nd edn, London

Sbordone, F. (1970) *Strabonis Geographica II: libri iii-vi.* Rome

Serra Ridgway, F. R. (1991) 'Etruscan art and culture: a bibliography 1978–1990', *Journal of Roman Archaeology* 4: 5–27

Shefton, B. B. (1982) 'Greeks and Greek imports in the south of the Iberian peninsula', in *PIW*, 337–70

Snodgrass, A. M. (1965) 'Barbarian Europe and Early Iron Age Greece', *Proceedings of the Prehistoric Society* 31: 229–40

(1977) *Archaeology and the rise of the Greek state.* Cambridge

(1980) 'Towards the interpretation of the Geometric figure-scenes', *Athenische Mitteilungen* 95: 51–8

(1982) 'Les origines du culte des héros dans la Grèce antique', in *MM*, 107–19

(1983) 'Two demographic notes', in *Renaissance* 167–71

(1987) *An Archaeology of Greece: the present state and future scope of a discipline* (Sather Classical Lectures 53). Berkeley CA/London (see Popham 1990)

(1988) 'The archaeology of the hero', *Annali, Istituto Orientale, Napoli: Archeologia e Storia Antica* 10: 19–26

(1989) 'The coming of the Iron Age in Greece: Europe's earliest Bronze/Iron transition', in M. L. S. Sørensen and R. Thomas (eds.), *The Bronze Age – Iron*

*Age transition in Europe* (British Archaeological Reports, International Series 483), 22–35. Oxford

Stoop, M. W. (1955) 'Some observations on the recent excavations on Ischia', *Antiquity and Survival* 4: 255–64

Taylour, Lord William (1958) *Mycenaean pottery in Italy and adjacent areas.* Cambridge

Teixidor, J. (1979) 'Bulletin d'épigraphie sémitique 1978–79, *Syria* 56: 353–405

Themelis, P. G. (1983) 'An eighth-century goldsmith's workshop at Eretria', in *Renaissance*, 157–65

Tiné, S. and Vagnetti, L. (1967) *I Micenei in Italia.* Fasano (Catalogue of the exhibition mounted in the Taranto National Museum on the occasion of the First International Congress of Mycenaean Studies, Rome)

Toms, J. (1986) 'The relative chronology of the Villanovan cemetery of Quattro Fontanili at Veii', *Annali, Istituto Orientale, Napoli: Archeologia e Storia Antica* 8: 41–97

Torelli, M. (1965) 'Un uovo di struzzo dipinto conservato nel museo di Tarquinia', *Studi Etruschi* 33: 329–65

Trendall, A. D. (1967) 'Archaeology in South Italy and Sicily, 1964–66', *Archaeological Reports for 1966–67*, 29–46

Tronchetti, C. (1979) 'Per la cronologia del *tophet* di Sant'Antioco', *Rivista di Studi Fenici* 7: 201–5

Vagnetti, L. (1970) 'I Micenei in Italia: la documentazione archeologica', *Parola del Passato* 25: 359–80

(1980) 'Mycenaean imports in central Italy', Appendix II in E. Peruzzi, *Mycenaeans in early Latium* (Incunabula Graeca 75), 151–67. Rome

(1982) ed., *Magna Grecia e mondo miceneo: nuovi documenti.* Taranto (Catalogue of the exhibition mounted in the Taranto National Museum on the occasion of the XXII Convegno di Studi sulla Magna Grecia)

(1989) 'A Sardinian askos from Crete', *Annual of the British School at Athens* 84: 355–60

Vagnetti, L. and Jones, R. E. (1988) 'Towards the identification of local Mycenaean pottery in Italy', in *Problems in Greek Prehistory* (Papers presented at the Centenary Conference of the British School at Athens, Manchester 1986), 335–48. Bristol

Vagnetti, L. and Lo Schiavo, F. (1989) 'Late Bronze Age long distance trade in the Mediterranean: the role of the Cypriots', in E. Peltenburg (ed.), *Early Society in Cyprus*, 217–43. Edinburgh

Vermeule, E. (1979) *Aspects of death in early Greek art and poetry.* Berkeley/Los Angeles/London

von Luschan, F. and Andrae, W. (1943) *Ausgrabungen in Sendschirli v: Die Kleinfunde.* Berlin

Ward Perkins, J. B. (1961) 'Veii. The historical topography of the ancient city', *Papers of the British School at Rome* 29: 1–123

Webster, T. B. L. (1958) *From Mycenae to Homer.* London

Whitehouse, R. D. (1973) 'The earliest towns in peninsular Italy', in C. Renfrew (ed.), *The explanation of culture change: models in prehistory*, 617–24. London

Whitley, J. (1988) 'Early states and hero cults: a reappraisal', *Journal of Hellenic Studies* 108: 173–82

Williams, D. (1986) 'Greek potters and their descendants in Campania and Southern Etruria, *c.* 720–630 BC', in J. Swaddling (ed.), *Italian Iron Age artefacts in the British Museum*, 295–304. London

Zancani Montuoro, P. (1971) 'Coppa di bronzo sbalzata', *Atti e Memorie della Società Magna Grecia* 11–12: 9–33

(1976) 'Tre notabili Enotrii dell'VIII secolo a.C.', *Atti e Memorie della Società Magna Grecia* 15–17: 9–82

# Index